IN THE COCKPIT

IN THE COCKPIT

INSIDE 50 HISTORY-MAKING AIRCRAFT

PHOTOGRAPHY BY ERIC F. LONG AND MARK A. AVINO

TEXT BY DANA BELL FOREWORD BY JOHN TRAVOLTA

COLLINS | DESIGN

An Imprint of HarperCollinsPublishers

In the Cockpit: Inside 50 History-Making Aircraft

Copyright © 2007 by the SMITHSONIAN INSTITUTION

HarperCollins books may be purchased for educational, business, or sales promotional use.
For information, please write: Special Markets Department, HarperCollins Publishers,
10 East 53rd Street, New York, NY 10022.

First published in 2007 by:
Collins Design,
An Imprint of HarperCollins*Publishers*
10 East 53rd Street
New York, NY 10022
Tel: (212) 207-7000
Fax: (212) 207-7654
collinsdesign@harpercollins.com
www.harpercollins.com

Distributed throughout the world by:
HarperCollins*Publishers*
10 East 53rd Street
New York, NY 10022
Fax: (212) 207-7654

Design by Lonewolfblacksheep

Library of Congress Control Number: 2006938541

ISBN: 978-0-06-114381-6
ISBN-10: 0-06-114381-2

Printed in China
10 11 12 13 SCP 10 9 8 7 6

This book is dedicated to the individuals who designed, built, maintained, tested, piloted, and preserved these aircraft. The images presented here are an acknowledgment of their commitment and success.

IN THE COCKPIT

CONTENTS

If it is true that the soul of a man sits near the head of the human body, it could also be true that a pilot sitting in a cockpit—using the intricate and often sophisticated instruments and machinery to accomplish miracles of space and distance—could be the soul of an aircraft.

In this book I found myself transported through the history of pilots' souls and what they were looking at while making a certain type of magic happen through the genius of flight.

Every cockpit has a personality that influences the pilot, beckoning him to explore the skies with whatever advances or limitations the years brought. Whether commanding the Wright Brothers 1903 Flyer or the Concorde, one just wants to be invited to experience all that flight offers. A pilot has in his blood a kind of spring fever of the skies that takes him wherever he wants to go.

—JOHN TRAVOLTA

As we begin our second volume of cockpit photography at the National Air and Space Museum, we again have to consider just how awesome this experience is. We are representing the history of aviation through the lenses of our cameras, using creative lighting to express what we believe best describes the thrill of flight. In working with museum artifacts, we believe it is most important to preserve the originality of the artifact, which means taking unusually careful measures—when setting up the camera, using lights that emit heat, and employing any other tools inside the cockpit—to ensure we get the shot without damage to the artifact. Each cockpit has been specially prepped for us by our Collections Specialists, who have cleaned and made sure we are safe from exposure to radioactive paint used on the dials of many of the cockpits. Much of the cleaning was done after museum hours, sometimes taking days to prepare. We have made these cockpits glow, but only after Collections has made them shine.

We begin where we left off, shooting film for this project. We are now using a Cambo Wide DS camera, the second generation of the camera we used previously. This camera has the advantage of a 38XLmm Schneider Super Angulon lens, designed to cover 6x7cm with plenty of shifts. We have used it to cover 4x5cm without the shifts, giving us the equivalence of a 12mm lens on a 35mm format. Again, we experience the distortion of extreme wide-angle lenses, making many of the cockpits look spacious, when they are not. Shooting extremely wide also allows us to pull in more information side to side and gives us plenty of room to crop from the top and/or bottom. In some cases, where the inside of the plane is rounded, as with the radio position in the Heinkel 219 or the cockpit of *SpaceShipOne*, we used a Mamiya RZII Pro or Hassleblad with a fish-eye lens. Our film is Kodak 64T tungsten or Kodak 100G daylight depending upon our control of the ambient light, and Polaroid Type 55 film, which offers us the luxury of a print (from which we can evaluate composition) and a negative (that we can study with a loupe to review sharpness). My preference is to use Mole Richardson Mini Mole tungsten lighting, which is smaller, thus making it easier to control, especially when adding light to shadow.

We are often asked why we have not switched to digital. While digital has its advantages—similar lens coverage; the ability to record a longer tonal range when shooting RAW files; no reliance on film, processing, and Polaroids—digital comes at an extremely high price. In addition to the cost of the equipment, there is the archiving of the image. Our standards for film preservation at the Smithsonian guarantee that color transparency film can last hundreds of years. With digital, it all depends upon the media to which it is saved, how archival it is, and what it can be read on years from now.

—ERIC F. LONG & MARK A. AVINO

This book showcases the cockpits of 50 aircraft from the collections of the Smithsonian Institution's National Air and Space Museum. Each cockpit, beautifully photographed by NASM photographers Eric Long and Mark Avino, has been preserved by the National Air and Space Museum to remind us of the evolution of aviation technology. Some may remind you, the reader, of aircraft you've flown for many hours; others, perhaps, will introduce you to aircraft you've never heard of.

We use the term *cockpit* somewhat in the common sense of a place where the aircraft is controlled. A quick perusal will show many changes in cockpit controls and instrumentation as aircraft grew more sophisticated or more specialized. We have selected our photos and text to give a general sense of how things worked and how aviators perceived the part of the aircraft often called "the office."

The Wrights taught the world that an airplane needed to be steered on three axes, but, with no single intuitive system, each pioneer seemed to create his own system of controls. Boats and automobiles were using a wheel or bar to turn left or right (yaw), so some early aircraft used three wheels or bars—not much of a solution for the normal, two-handed pilot. In America, the Wrights installed a left-hand stick for pitch (nose up and down) and one or two right-hand sticks for roll (raising one wingtip, depressing the other) and yaw. The other common American system, designed by Curtiss, controlled roll with a shoulder harness, pitch with a stick, and yaw with a wheel mounted at the tip of the stick.

Neither of those systems would remain in use past 1918. The same is true of a lesser-known system patented by American inventor James Henry Joyce. Joyce mounted a wheel at the end of a control stick (similar to the Curtiss system) but controlled pitch by pulling or pushing the stick, roll by moving it laterally, and yaw by turning the wheel. Although the Joyce Stick Controls saw little use, they may have morphed in the common name for a control stick when the Joyce Stick became the Joy Stick.

The French would devise the two most common control systems in use today. Louis Blériot was responsible for the introduction of rudder pedals and a familiar control stick, while Armand Deperdussin created the system of stick, wheel, and rudder pedals that were known as Dep Controls into the 1920s.

Regardless of the system of controls or number of instruments, we hope you'll have a seat in your favorite armchair and enjoy stunning pictures of some of the most memorable aircraft in aviation history. Whether you're on a nostalgic visit to an old "office" or being introduced to a fascinating new aeronautical artifact, we think you'll be entertained and enlightened.

—DANA BELL

WRIGHT BROTHERS 1903 FLYER

Few realized it at the time, but the world changed on December 17, 1903. On that day, brothers Orville and Wilbur Wright made four flights in their Flyer, the first successful, powered, heavier-than-air flying machine. For some time, aeronauts had navigated the skies in unpowered gliders, free balloons, and dirigible airships, but the Wrights' machine made the leap in aerodynamics and technology that launched a new aerial age.

Development of the Wrights' 1903 aircraft began in 1899, the concept growing from the brothers' experiences with a five-foot biplane kite to a program of innovative wind tunnel experiments and three piloted gliders. The third glider proved remarkably successful; with more than 700 test flights in 1902, it provided the Wrights with valuable engineering experience while also teaching them how to fly. Its final design, coupled with a 12 horsepower gasoline engine, formed the basis of the first engine-powered machine.

The 1903 Flyer was first flown by Orville, who lay prone across the lower wing, his feet braced on a wooden bar. He had only three flight controls. The first, a clip at the wing's leading edge, was released with the right hand to send the aircraft down a wooden launch rail. The second, a lever held in the left hand, controlled the elevators that made the plane climb and dive. The last was a hip cradle, wired to twist the wings while turning the twin rudders; shifting the cradle laterally turned the aircraft left or right. The pilot had no throttle, as the engine was adjusted on the ground prior to flight.

The 1903 Flyer carried three instruments, all meant to be read after each flight. Started simultaneously as the aircraft traveled down the launch rail, the engine revolution counter, anemometer, and stopwatch were shut off as the aircraft touched down. When combined with measurements of wind speed and flight distance, the instruments could help calculate air speed, ground speed, and engine revolutions per minute.

WILBUR WRIGHT ATTEMPTED THE FIRST FLIGHT OF THE

WRIGHT 1903 FLYER ON DECEMBER 14. THE BROTHERS QUICKLY

REPAIRED THE DAMAGED PLANE, AND THREE DAYS LATER,

ORVILLE QUICKLY MADE THE FIRST SUCCESSFUL FLIGHT.

TODAY THE WRIGHT BROTHERS' 1903 FLYER IS ON

DISPLAY IN A PLACE OF HONOR IN THE NATIONAL AIR

AND SPACE MUSEUM IN WASHINGTON, D.C.

WRIGHT BROTHERS 1909 MILITARY FLYER

On August 2, 1909, the Wright 1909 Military Flyer, the world's first military airplane, was accepted into service by the U.S. Army as *Signal Corps No.1*. The two-seat observation and training aircraft was built in response to the Army's 1908 request for an airplane that could carry two at a speed of 40 mph, remain airborne for at least one hour, and cover a distance of 125 miles.

The Wrights' first entry in this competition was successfully demonstrated at Fort Myer, Virginia, for two weeks in September 1908. Then, on September 17, a prop blade split in flight, causing a crash that injured Orville Wright and killed his passenger, Army Lt. Thomas E. Selfridge. The lieutenant was the first crash fatality in a viable heavier-than-air airplane.

The Wrights returned the next summer with a new aircraft that successfully completed all flight trials, earning a purchase price of $25,000 plus a $5,000 bonus for exceeding the speed requirement by 2 mph. *Signal Corps No.1* would enter Army service as a flight trainer at College Park, Maryland, and Fort Sam Houston, Texas. The introduction of newer and safer aircraft designs limited the aircraft to less than two years' service before it was transferred to the Smithsonian Institution in 1911.

The crew of the 1909 Military Flyer sat side by side at the leading edge of the lower wing. (After nearly being thrown from the aircraft on March 12, 1910, Lt. Benjamin D. Foulois would add a 4-foot strap, the first military safety belt.) To the left, the pilot held an elevator control stick in his left hand; the student/observer held a similar lever in his right hand. Between them, one shared lever controlled rudders and wing warping; fore-and-aft movement for the rudders, lateral for wing warping, and diagonal for both. This lever was later replaced by two sticks that could be held in one hand; in a control system similar to other early Wright aircraft, one stick operated the rudder; the other, the wing warping.

A small degree of engine control was introduced with a single foot pedal between the two crew members. While not a true throttle, the pedal controlled magneto sparking and so the rate of ignition firing.

There were no flight instruments, though an 8-inch string on a crossbar ahead of the aviators served as a rudimentary yaw indicator.

ORVILLE WRIGHT ADJUSTS THE MOTOR ON THE WRIGHT 1909 MILITARY FLYER PRIOR TO A TEST FLIGHT AT FORT MYER, VIRGINIA.

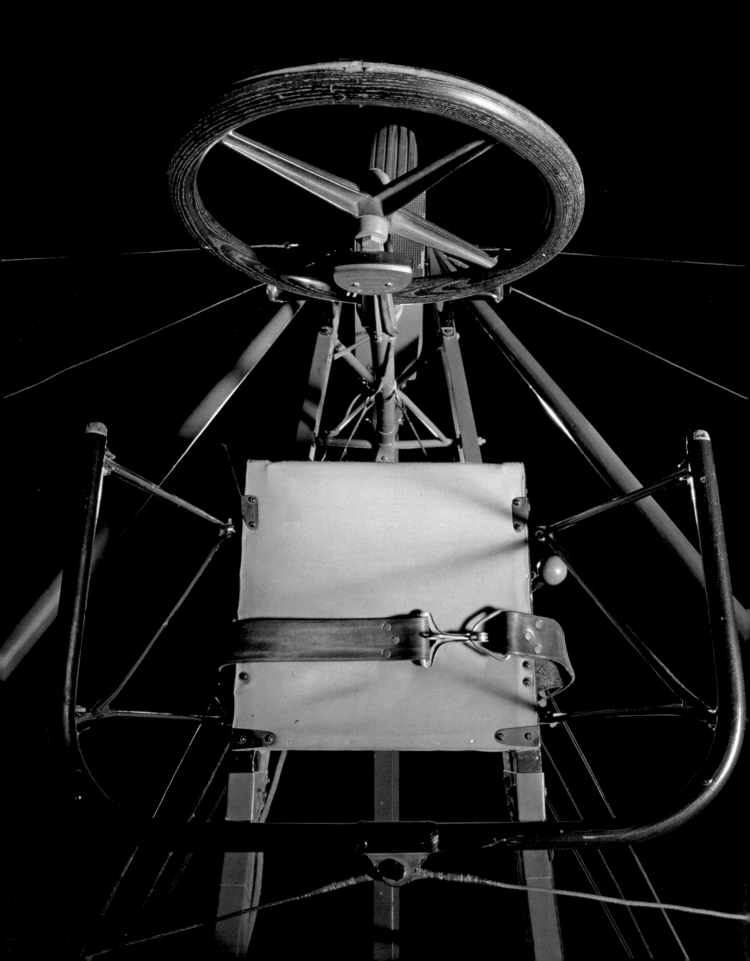

CURTISS MODEL D HEADLESS PUSHER

The early pushers of aviation pioneer Glenn H. Curtiss were among the most successful aircraft of their day. Mounted on pontoons, they became the first seaplanes and amphibious aircraft; built with enclosed hulls, they gave birth to a line of flying boats. The Curtiss Pushers would win prizes and trophies throughout the U.S. and Europe, and their design would be imitated by countless would-be aeronauts.

At the beginning of the 1900s, as the Wrights were building their first gliders, Glenn Curtiss designed his first lightweight motorcycle engines, and he built a reputation as a daredevil motorcycle racer. Curtiss began his aeronautical work in 1904, helping fit his engines to "Captain" Thomas Scott Baldwin's dirigibles. A year later, he met Dr. Alexander Graham Bell, joining Bell's Aerial Experiment Association (AEA) as chief executive officer and director of experiments in 1907. After designing four airplanes (including the first to fly in the British Empire), the AEA disbanded in early 1909. Bell continued to dabble in aeronautics, but chief engineer F. W. "Casey" Baldwin and assistant engineer John A. D. McCurdy joined forces to create the Curtiss aircraft company.

As seen from above, the Curtiss flight controls might seem familiar to modern observers, though there were important differences. As on today's aircraft, fore-and-aft movement of the control moved the elevators. (Early Curtiss pushers had one elevator in the front and another in the rear. With the forward elevator removed, the aircraft were called *headless pushers*.) The wheel itself, which today is linked to the ailerons, controlled the rudder. The ailerons were linked to a pilot's shoulder harness; a lean to the left or right banked the aircraft in that direction.

With years of engine experience, Curtiss ensured that most of his aircraft were equipped with a throttle, which was mounted just to the right of the seat on this aircraft. The Pushers rarely carried flight or engine instruments.

The Curtiss control system remained a standard into 1917. With the United States gearing up for World War I, the need for uniform systems and training forced the adoption of European-style control sticks and rudder pedals. At the same time, all throttles were ordered moved to the pilot's left.

ALTHOUGH THE CURTISS MODEL D WOULD BE SURPASSED BY NEWER DESIGNS BEFORE WORLD WAR I, GLENN CURTISS BUILT THIS FINAL HEADLESS PUSHER IN 1919.

ECKER FLYING BOAT

The success of Glenn Curtiss' early aircraft inspired many imitators, including Herman A. Ecker. This Syracuse, New York, native, who probably learned to fly in 1911, quickly became involved with several aircraft construction projects. In 1912 or 1913, he built a flying boat copied from the Curtiss F Boat.

One of hundreds of pioneer aircraft built for private use, Ecker's Flying Boat was a "homebuilt" long before that term came into popular use. Like so many of his contemporaries, Ecker worked independently, copying a sound design but using substandard materials and building methods. Most internal bracing was omitted—Ecker may have been unaware of its use in the professionally manufactured Curtiss aircraft. The muslin covering was secured with carpet tacks and sealed with wallpaper glue and varnish. Ecker converted a six-cylinder Roberts marine engine for aeronautical use. Hardware and fittings came from the local hardware store or were jury-rigged from other materials. Despite the amateur nature of its construction, the aircraft served its builder well, flying safely for three years before being retired to storage.

The wide-open cockpit of the Ecker Flying Boat provided a comfortable bench seat for the pilot and one passenger. Although later Curtiss boats carried a heavy diagonal brace between the pilot and passenger (to prevent the engine from tumbling into the cockpit on a crash landing), Ecker may have been unaware of this modification. The Roberts marine engine featured a hand-crank starter, turned from the cockpit before flight, and Ecker added a foot throttle to regulate his speed. There were no engine instruments; the pilot simply listened to the roar behind his head for any hint of a problem.

The control system was the original Curtiss type, with shoulder harness and steering wheel. Most of Ecker's flights were short, limited by fuel capacity to about a half hour. The lack of flight instruments was not unusual at the time, and Ecker had few problems navigating between his air show appearances in central and western New York State.

AFTER ALMOST 70 YEARS IN STORAGE, THE ECKER FLYING BOAT WAS RESTORED BY THE STAFF OF THE NATIONAL AIR AND SPACE MUSEUM IN 1982.

SEVERAL WORLD WAR I HALBERSTADTS WERE SET ASIDE FOR USE AS SMALL POSTWAR AIRLINERS.

THREE COMPLETE EXAMPLES HAVE BEEN RESTORED FROM THE SURVIVING COMPONENTS.

HALBERSTADT CL.IV

The German "CL" aircraft class, introduced in autumn 1917, was a family of light, maneuverable ground-attack aircraft. The Halberstadt CL.II, a design from Halberstadter Flugzeug-Werke GmbH, proved one of the most effective of the class, leading to the introduction of the Halberstadt CL.IV in March 1918. The Germans took advantage of the new aircraft's speed and maneuverability to dodge ground fire while bringing pressure to bear on Allied ground forces during the 1918 spring offensive. When the German's offensive failed, the CL.IV moved to defensive ground-support missions, two-seat fighter-escort missions, and night bombing raids.

The Halberstadt's plywood fuselage included a single, elongated cockpit shared by the two crew members. The pilot sat on a bench seat atop the 35-liter main fuel tank, with the observer/gunner close behind on a canvas strap. Both crew members had excellent visibility, particularly over the close-set upper wing. Each Halberstadt CL.IV was wired for a radio, with leads for electrically heated flying suits, though neither installation saw much wartime use.

The pilot's two-handed control stick carried triggers for one or two Spandau machine guns, if they were mounted. A gauge to the right of the seat measured the fuel below; pumps moved the fuel to a gravity tank in the wing above. Reports of captured Halberstadts generally noted an instrument panel with starting magneto, main switch, gas pressure gauges, oil pressure gauges, air pump, level indicator, and airspeed indicator. Other instruments were often mounted outside the cockpit: a tachometer was set into the windshield; a coolant thermometer set into a radiator line farther forward; a barograph (simple altimeter), between left interplane struts; and a floating compass, set in the left lower wing.

When a radio was mounted, it was operated by the gunner, who was also responsible for dropping anti-personnel hand grenades, launching signal flares, and firing his defensive Parabellum machine gun.

FOKKER T-2

On May 3, 1923, a Fokker T-2 piloted by U.S. Army Air Service Lt. Oakley G. Kelly and Lt. John A. Macready became the first aircraft to make a nonstop flight across North America.

In 1922, the U.S. Army had ordered a pair of large transports from Dutch manufacturer Anthony Fokker. He improved on his successful F.III airliner, enlarging the standard Fokker cantilevered plywood monoplane wing, adding a single American 420-horse-power Liberty V-12 engine, and building a cabin large enough to carry ten passengers and their baggage. The two aircraft were designated F.IV in Fokker records and T-2 in the Air Service's new designation system.

The Air Service quickly recognized that the T-2 could be modified to carry enough fuel for the coast-to-coast flight. The center wing section was strengthened, and the 130-gallon fuel capacity was increased to 725 gallons. After two unsuccessful attempts at the cross-country flight, Kelly and Macready took off from Long Island, New York, on May 2, 1923. With an average ground speed of only 92 mph, the trip to Rockwell Field, California, took almost 27 hours.

The T-2 may have been large, but its open cockpit was not. A single pilot sat forward of the plywood wing, just to the left of the Liberty engine, which produced power, heat, noise, and a fine spray of oil. The throttle and mixture controls were mounted to the pilot's right, fixed to the left cylinder bank. Flight gauges on the rudimentary instrument panel comprised a compass, altimeter, airspeed indicator, and turn and bank indicator. For the record flight, a second set of controls and instruments was added in the cabin, allowing the relief pilot to take control (although with no forward visibility), while the pilot made in-flight engine adjustments. Rest periods were important on the long flight, but switching positions was a complicated affair. From behind the cockpit, the relief pilot would first remove the pilot's seatback and parachute, then take over the auxiliary controls. The pilot then lifted his hinged seat bottom, crawled into the cabin, and traded places as the relief pilot moved forward. Kelly and Macready made this switch four times, once at night.

TYPICAL OF THE NEW, LARGE TRANSPORTS INTRODUCED AFTER WORLD WAR I, THE FOKKER T-2'S ENCLOSED CABIN PROVIDED A MODICUM OF COMFORT FOR ITS PASSENGERS, WHILE ITS PILOT FLEW IN AN OPEN COCKPIT.

ARROW SPORT A2-60

The Arrow Aircraft and Motors Corporation rolled out its first Arrow Sport A2-60 in 1926. Weekend pilots would make the Arrow Sport one of the United States' most popular pre-Depression aircraft. Doped fabric covered a welded steel tube fuselage and spruce and plywood cantilever wing—a framework so sturdy that interplane N struts would be added more for pilot confidence than for any structural requirements. The wide-track, split-axle landing gear improved stability for landing and taxiing. A 60-horsepower engine provided enough power for the average user, and a factory-delivered price tag of $2,900 to $3,485 made the Arrow Sport a bargain for most new aircraft buyers.

The Arrow Sport shown here was built in February 1929 but continued to fly, with some modifications, until May 1983. Of the handful of cockpit upgrades added in that half century, several have been removed, leaving most instruments in their original configuration. Built at a time when most private aircraft featured tandem seating, the Arrow Sport positioned its pilot and passenger side-by-side. This shared cockpit, which featured excellent visibility, dual control sticks locked together by steel tubing, and two sets of rudder pedals, resulted in a comfortable training aircraft, though the single throttle was available only to the pilot in the left seat.

The center oval instrument panel, easy for both pilots to see, comprised an airspeed indicator, engine temperature and oil temperature gauges, and an altimeter. The tachometer (at the extreme right), gas gauge (to the right below the center panel), voltmeter (to the left above the throttle), and second altimeter (above the voltmeter) were later additions in this Arrow Sport's flying career. Thus, the original

instrumentation can be seen as rudimentary at best. With no navigational instruments—not even a compass—any attempt at cross-country flying required discernable landmarks. Likewise, without blind-flying instrumentation and cockpit lighting, the Arrow Sport could not safely attempt flying at night. Lack of a radio meant that pilots communicated with other aircraft or flying fields through maneuver and hand signals. Although a bit rough by today's standards, the Arrow Sport represents a comfortable norm for contemporary open cockpits.

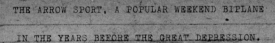

THE ARROW SPORT, A POPULAR WEEKEND BIPLANE

IN THE YEARS BEFORE THE GREAT DEPRESSION.

LOCKHEED 5B VEGA
"LITTLE RED BUS"

Introduced in 1927, the Lockheed Vega led two lives. A favorite small airliner and transport, the Vega was also the choice for many attempting distance, speed, and altitude records. The Vega used a plywood cantilever wing (of similar construction to the Fokker design) with a molded plywood monocoque fuselage.

One of the many pilots who appreciated the Vega's qualities was Amelia Earhart. In November 1929, she had used one to set a women's speed record over a 1-mile course. At the controls of another, she set two more women's speed records in June 1930. At that time, Earhart already owned another Vega, a 15-month-old Lockheed demonstrator that she was quietly having modified for long-distance flights.

In 1928, Earhart had become famous as the first woman to fly across the Atlantic, but she had been frustrated by her passenger status on that flight. Her bright red Vega 5B, which she referred to as the *Little Red Bus*, was to end that frustration. On May 20, 1932,

Earhart took off from Harbor Grace, Newfoundland. When she landed near Culmore, Londonderry, Northern Ireland, almost 15 hours later, she had become the first woman to pilot an aircraft across the Atlantic and only the second person to make the flight alone.

Earhart was not through with the *Little Red Bus*, however. On August 24 and 25, 1932, she flew the Vega from Los Angeles, California, to Newark, New Jersey, making the first solo nonstop transcontinental flight by a woman.

Each of the 128 Vegas was built by hand, and each enclosed cockpit was configured to match the customer's needs and budget. The *Little Red Bus* cockpit was more sophisticated than most, having been modified for navigation and safety on long-distance flights. Blind-flying instruments dominated the center of the panel, while separate gauges monitored the remaining fuel in each tank, and a flow meter measured fuel consumption in gallons per hour.

WHETHER SETTING RECORDS OR HAULING FREIGHT, THE LOCKHEED VEGA WAS A SLEEK, CLEAN DESIGN.

EARHART'S *LITTLE RED BUS* WAS THE TWENTY-SECOND VEGA BUILT IN A TOTAL PRODUCTION RUN OF 128 AIRCRAFT.

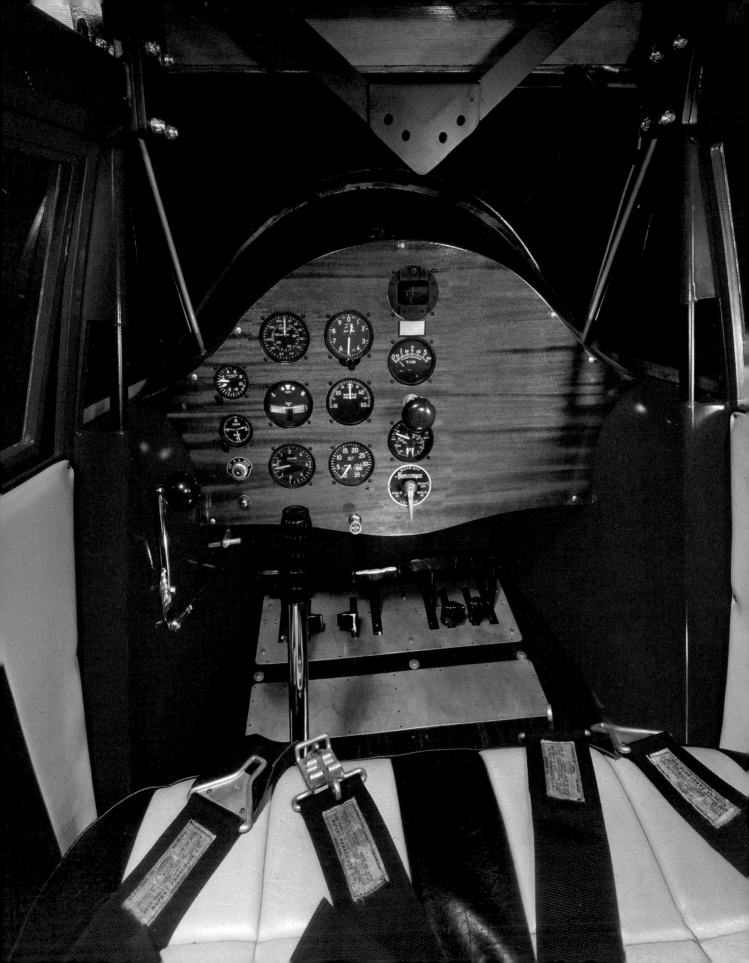

LITTLE BUTCH, AN AEROBATIC VERSION OF THE POPULAR MONOCOUPE BUSINESS LIGHT PLANE.

MONOCOUPE 110 SPECIAL "LITTLE BUTCH"

W.W. Edmondson and his Monocoupe 110 Special *Little Butch* won the first International Aerobatics Championships, held in 1948.

The first Monocoupe was built 20 years earlier when Don Luscombe designed a light, two-place "monoplane coupe" for personal or business use. With side-by-side seating and an enclosed cabin, the Monocoupe was a comfortable alternative to contemporary open-cockpit biplanes. By the end of 1928, almost 90 percent of all the light planes produced and sold in the United States were Monocoupes.

With a 110-horsepower Warner Scarab radial engine, the Model 110 was already a peppy aircraft when the first 110 Special appeared in 1932. That's when pilot Johnny Livingston asked the factory to produce a pylon racing version with shorter wingspan, reduced tail planes, and a 145-horsepower Warner Scarab.

Of the 350 or so Monocoupes built, only ten would be Specials. One of these, built in early 1941, was too hot for its first three owners; two had accidents and the third sold the aircraft after just seven months. In March 1944, Woody Edmondson became the fourth owner, purchasing it for transportation between his wartime flying schools. The aircraft's short nose gave it a bulldoglike appearance, so he named it *Little Butch*.

After World War II, Edmondson upgraded the power plant for aerobatic flying and entered the air show circuit. Competitively, Edmondson placed second at the Miami Air Maneuvers in 1946 and in 1947; he then placed first in the 1948 International Aerobatics Championships. He continued to fly *Little Butch* in air shows until 1951, selling the aircraft in 1960.

The Monocoupe's comfortable cockpit offered pilot and passenger a business-suit environment with car-door entrances at either side. Although dual controls could be fitted, the aircraft was designed to fly from the left seat, and only one throttle was installed. The panel included basic navigational instruments (though the stresses of acrobatic flight precluded use of an artificial horizon), and engine and fuel gauges in no particular order. To the left, Edmondson mounted an accelerometer to keep track of g-forces during his aerobatic routines.

BÜCKER BÜ 133C JUNGMEISTER

First flown in 1935, the German Bücker Bü 133 Jungmeister (Young Champion) was, and still is, one of the world's finest single-seat aerobatic biplanes. Descended from the Bü 131 trainer, the Jungmeister was enthusiastically accepted by flying clubs all over Europe (where it dominated the aerobatic scene), and by the pre-World War II German Luftwaffe. The most widely produced version was the Bü 133 C, which was powered by a seven-cylinder, 160-horsepower Siemens radial engine.

The Bü 133 C depicted here was first owned by Romanian aerobatic pilot Alex Papana, who demonstrated the aircraft's capabilities inside the track and field stadium at the 1936 Berlin Olympics. Later that year, Papana shipped the Jungmeister to the U.S. as freight on the German airship *Hindenburg*. In 1937, both he and German aerobatic champion Count Otto von Hagenburg flew the aircraft competitively at the Cleveland Air Races. Then in 1938, Mike Murphy flew it to win the American Aerobatic Champion-ship at the Miami All American Air Maneuvers. After Papana had an accident in 1940, Murphy bought the aircraft and rebuilt it with a Warner engine, again taking the American Aerobatic Championship later that year.

The Jungmeister was subsequently sold to Beverly "Bevo" Howard, who flew it to victory in the 1946 and 1947 aerobatic championships (besting Woody Edmondson in *Little Butch*). Howard continued to fly demonstrations in the aircraft until October 17, 1971, when he crashed at a Charleston, South Carolina, air show. Howard died in the crash, but his friends and family rebuilt the famous Jungmeister as a fitting memorial. They donated it to the National Air and Space Museum.

The Jungmeister's cockpit was a tight fit for most pilots. Side panels folded down for entry then closed over the pilot's shoulders. The instrument panel on Howard's plane showed a mix of original German gauges (rate of climb, air speed) and American replacements.

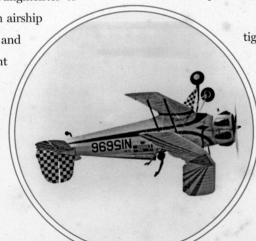

AEROBATIC CHAMPION "BEVO" HOWARD, DEMONSTRATING THE JUNGMEISTER IN INVERTED FLIGHT.

A TRIO OF N3N-3S IN FLIGHT SHORTLY BEFORE WORLD WAR II. FORMATION FLIGHT WAS NOT PART OF THE N3N

STUDENT CURRICULUM, SUGGESTING THAT THESE AIRCRAFT ARE FLOWN BY INSTRUCTORS.

NAVAL AIRCRAFT FACTORY N3N-3

First flying in 1936, Naval Aircraft Factory N3N would train naval aviators for a quarter century. In 1960, the final example retired as the last biplane serving the U.S. military.

The Naval Aircraft Factory (NAF) had been established at the Philadelphia Navy Yard in 1917. As a government facility, the NAF was initially responsible for exploring developments in aeronautical technology, monitoring aircraft construction costs, and building a portion of the Navy's aircraft inventory. While most of the aircraft built there between 1918 and 1945 were licensed variations of other designs, the N3N came from NAF's own engineers, and all 997 examples were built at its own facility.

The N3N was an *ab initio* (primary) trainer, designed to prepare prospective naval aviators for more complicated aircraft. Under the Navy's 1941 syllabus, the naval aviation cadet's first flight instruction involved ten hours of elimination flying (to "wash out" the unfit) and a first solo flight. Next came about 70 of primary training in an N3N (or similar aircraft), followed by almost 30 hours in a basic trainer (learning more complicated systems and formation flying). With an additional 18 hours of instrument training and blind flying and 85 hours of specialized training, the cadet would graduate, earning his naval aviator's wings of gold.

Each Navy primary trainer, including the N3N, was painted a bright orange-yellow to avoid collisions. Learning the controls, the Navy's least-qualified flyers posed a danger to themselves, their instructors, and anyone else in range. These aircraft soon earned the nickname Yellow Peril.

Seated in the aft cockpit, the instructor could watch his student's progress, communicating through a one-way Gosport (linking the instructor's voice directly to the student's ear). Flight controls were permanently linked, and an instructor could find himself wrestling with any student who would not release the stick when ordered. The simple instrument panel was adequate for the job at hand; more advanced instruments and controls would be waiting for those skilled enough to move to the next level of instruction.

THE CLASSIC LINES OF A J-3C IN FLIGHT OVER PENNSYLVANIA SHORTLY BEFORE WORLD WAR II.

PIPER J-3C CUB

For a generation of aviators, stories often begin with the words, "I had my first flight in a Piper Cub." Inexpensive, easy and fun to fly, the Cub began life late in 1930 when William T. Piper bought the bankrupt Taylor Company's name and assets and set the staff to work on a low-cost alternative to the Taylor Chummy light plane. With a cost of about $4,000, the Chummy was a difficult sale during the Great Depression and only ten would be produced. Piper wanted a smaller aircraft for half the price.

The new aircraft, designed by C. Gilbert Taylor was designated the E-2. The original 20-horse-power Brownbach Tiger Kitten engine didn't provide enough thrust for a test flight, but it did provide a name—Taylor's accountant suggested that an airplane with a Kitten engine should be known as a cub. Fitted with a new Continental engine, the Taylor E-2 Cub was a bargain at $1,325, but sales moved slowly for the first three years.

E-2 sales improved in 1934, and more than 200 new orders would be filled in 1935. That year, Piper had engineer Walter Corey Jamouneau redesign the Cub. With rounded wing tips and tail planes, a new cabin, and revised fuselage, the new Taylor Cub would be designated J-2 (J for Jamouneau). By 1937, more J-2 Cubs had been sold than any other private aircraft in American history—about 300 under the Taylor name and another 358 under the Piper Aircraft Corporation (as the company was known from June 1937). That year minor revisions led to the introduction of the J-3 Cub. The J-3 would become a popular trainer for civilian pilots through the end of World War II; there were also militarized versions serving in artillery-spotting and liaison roles. When the last J-3 was completed in 1947, more than 20,000 had been produced.

Economy had a major role in every part of the Cub's design, including the cockpit layout. Instrumentation was kept to a minimum, with a single front panel carrying the tachometer, oil temperature gauge, airspeed indicator, compass, oil pressure gauge, and altimeter standard on most aircraft. On solo flights, this placed the pilot a bit farther from the instruments than usual—for balance, solos had to be flown from the back seat!

TURNER-LAIRD LTR-14 "MISS CHAMPION"

With his handlebar moustache and dashing smile, Sam Browne belt and equestrian jodhpurs, and, of course, his pet lion, Gilmore, Roscoe Turner was the poster boy for all the flamboyant air-race pilots of the 1930s. But beyond the flash, this colonel of the nonexistent Nevada Air Force was a skilled and instinctive pilot and a gifted designer.

In 1936, Turner designed a racer that he called the Turner Special or RT-14 (Roscoe Turner, 14-cylinder engine). Unhappy with the RT-14's wing loading, he shipped the unflown aircraft to Emil Matthew "Matty" Laird for redesign. The rebuilt aircraft was rechristened the LTR-14 (Laird Turner Racer, 14-cylinder engine). Sponsored by Ring Free Oil, Turner named the LTR-14 *Ring Free Meteor* for the 1937 Thompson Trophy Race at the National Air Races. Leading for most of the short-course pylon race, Turner missed a pylon when he was blinded by the sun on the final lap; he finished third.

The Pump Engineering Service Corporation sponsored Turner and the LTR-14, now called the *Pesco Special*, for the 1938 Thompson race, which Turner won handily. With Champion Spark Plugs as sponsor, Turner renamed the LTR-14 *Miss Champion* before winning the 1939 Thompson. With a previous victory in 1934, Turner became the only three-time winner of the hotly contested Thompson race. (True to character, Turner refused to return the trophy when new, reorganized Thompson races were introduced after World War II.)

Turner sat low in the LTR-14's cockpit. Even with his seat raised for taxiing, his forward visibility was limited. The aircraft's long, aluminum-painted nose and large Pratt & Whitney Twin Wasp Senior Radial engine would contribute to his missing a pylon in the 1937 Thompson.

As might be expected, the instrument panel carried a sophisticated array of gauges for monitoring engine performance. The complete blind-flying panel, which seems out of place in a daytime pylon racer, suggests that Turner also had plans to use the LTR-14 for cross-country racing, plans that were never realized.

WITH HIS CANOPY RETRACTED AND SEAT RAISED, ROSCOE TURNER PEERS OVER THE LTR-14'S

WINGS AND FUSELAGE AT THE 1939 NATIONAL AIR RACES.

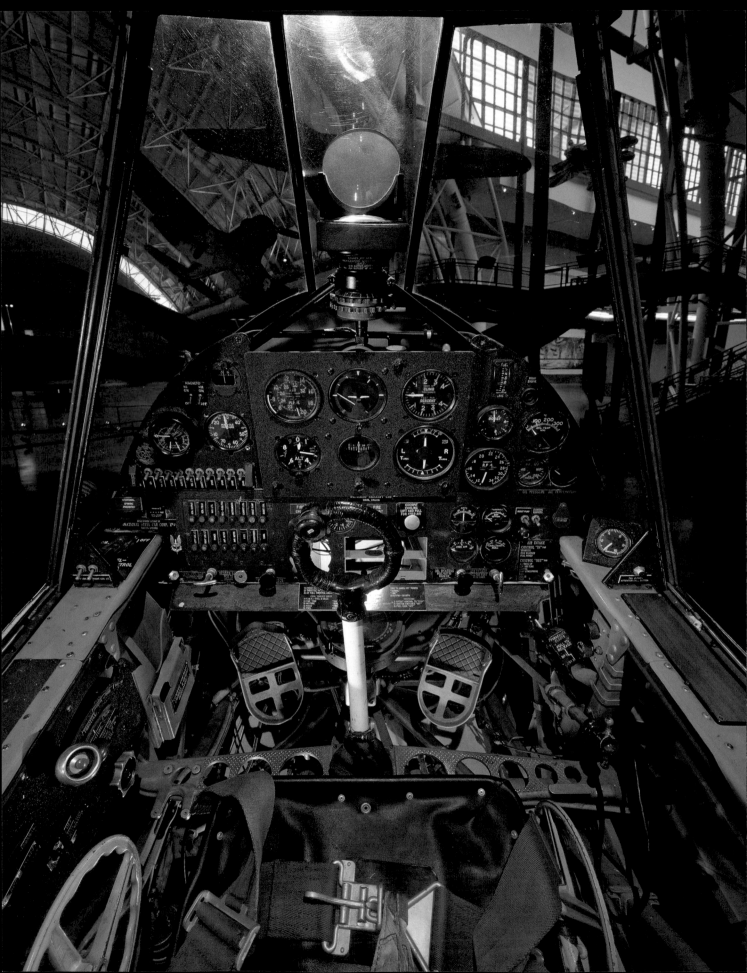

WESTLAND LYSANDER MARK III

The years leading up to World War II found many world military planners investing in single-engined, light attack and observation ground-support aircraft. Flying at low speeds and altitudes, the planes and their two- or three-man crews were supposed to harass enemy troops and emplacements with small antipersonnel bombs and light machine guns, while defending themselves from marauding fighters with an additional machine gun or two.

The Westland Lysander, which first flew in June 1936, was one such aircraft. As with nearly every aircraft of this type, the Lysander was too slow and too lightly armed, dooming it from its first encounter with modern air combat. During the Battle of France (May and June 1940), 174 Lysanders would face the German Luftwaffe; 88 would be shot down, with 30 more destroyed on the ground.

Through mid–1943, a few Lysanders flew combat missions in regions where there was little threat of enemy air action, primarily in parts of the Middle East and Far East. Most surviving Lysanders (and similar aircraft) were quickly assigned to secondary support roles such as target towing, air-sea rescue, and staff liaison.

But the "Lizzy," as the Lysander was known to its crews, was also the perfect aircraft for a role its designers could have never envisioned. The first operational British aircraft equipped with automatic leading edge slats and trailing edge flaps, the Lysander exhibited remarkable short takeoff or landing (STOL) capabilities. It was uniquely suited to flying agents in and out of small fields at night in occupied Europe, a mission it began in 1941.

In the cockpit, the pilot and gunner had exceptional visibility in nearly every direction. The pilot's blind flying panel was flanked by engine instruments and small switches, including an unusual Tail Gunner Attention Call Button mounted on the right canopy rail. The two-handed control stick was common in British aircraft of the period.

THE LYSANDER'S UNUSUAL WING PROVIDED EXCELLENT LIFT AND LOW-SPEED MANEUVERABILITY WHILE AFFORDING ITS CREW SUPERB VISIBILITY.

BOEING S-307
STRATOLINER
"CLIPPER FLYING CLOUD"

The first pressurized airliner cabin signaled a major advance in commercial air transportation. It was the Boeing 307 Stratoliner, first flying on December 31, 1938, that introduced this new technology to scheduled airline service.

Flight at higher altitudes allowed aircraft to achieve higher speeds and avoid the foul weather and turbulence often found below 10,000 feet. Supercharged engines, in use since the 1920s, gave aircraft the boost they needed to fly at those higher altitudes. But, above 10,000 feet, humans are less adaptable. The Boeing 307 used what was then known as a cabin supercharger to maintain a cabin pressure found at 8,000 feet, even when the aircraft was flying above 20,000 feet. With cabin heaters, passengers could ride in suit-coat comfort while speeding across the country.

The technological advances of the late 1930s often saw aircraft surpassed before they could even enter production. This had happened with the Douglas DC-4E, the first airliner designed for a pressurized cabin. A complex and expensive aircraft, the DC-4E would exist only as a prototype before Pan American and TWA shifted their orders to Boeing's Stratoliner, effectively killing the Douglas program.

Ten Stratoliners had been ordered (a prototype, three for Pan Am, five for TWA, and one for Howard Hughes) when Lockheed introduced its pressurized Constellation, which could carry a third more passengers more than 50 mph faster. There would

be no further Stratoliners built after Pan Am and TWA each ordered 40 of the new Constellations. The last Boeing 307s were still flying in the 1970s. (One aircraft, with wings and tail removed, was even converted to a houseboat.)

The 307's flight deck had been developed through the company's experiences with the Model 314 transatlantic flying boat and the B-17 bomber. The minimum crew consisted of a flight engineer, who monitored the engines, fuel, and cabin pressure, and two pilots. Each pilot had a complete blind flying panel and a full set of engine controls—including throttles. A Sperry autopilot was centered on the instrument board.

On most flights, the Stratoliner also carried two other crew members: a radio operator, seated behind the pilot, and a navigator, whose "office" was just behind the flight deck.

PAN AMERICAN NAMED MOST OF ITS AIRLINERS; THE *CLIPPER FLYING CLOUD* WAS ONE OF THREE STRATOLINERS FLOWN BY THE COMPANY.

HAWKER HURRICANE MARK IIC

When first unveiled in 1935, the British Hawker Hurricane marked a new standard in fighter design. One of the first modern military aircraft, the Hurricane was a monoplane featuring aluminum framework, fully retractable landing gear, retractable flaps, and an enclosed cockpit. A newly developed Rolls Royce Merlin engine gave it a top speed of more than 300 mph in level flight. The Hurricane carried eight rifle-caliber machine guns at a time when most fighters carried only two. By late 1940, the Hurricane Mark IIB mounted 12 machine guns; and in early 1941, the Mark IIC introduced four 20mm cannons.

The Hurricane's cockpit was a tight fit for most pilots: design doctrine then called for a small aircraft with a large engine. There was no floor (a weight-saving concession), but a pair of foot tracks were mounted between the seat and rudder pedals. Due to a number of prewar innovations, there were very few changes to the Hurricane's basic cockpit layout over its nine-year production run. In 1937, the Royal Air Force standardized the Basic Six arrangement of blind-flying instruments; the center panel in every British-produced aircraft comprised an identical arrangement of airspeed indicator, artificial horizon, rate-of-climb indicator, altimeter, directional gyro, and turn and bank indicator. A Mark II reflector gun sight, also standardized in 1939, projected above the panel, while a large aperiodic magnetic compass (common in most British military cockpits of the 1930s and 1940s) stood below the panel.

The Hurricane's design innovations required new controls. A single lever at the pilot's right knee moved through two parallel channels: the left channel retracted or lowered the landing gear, while the right channel controlled the flaps. Few pilots at the time were familiar with retractable landing gear, so Hawker installed a buzzer that sounded at lower airspeeds, warning if the gear had not yet been lowered; similar systems are still found in all aircraft with retractable landing gear. Simple switches for communication radios, pilot oxygen, and electrical heating for high-altitude flight suits were all arranged to the pilot's left. The sliding canopy over the pilot opened and closed manually, and, in an emergency, could be jettisoned with a pull of the red handle to the pilot's right. A twist of a single quick-release fitting then freed the Sutton harness shoulder straps and lap belts before the pilot bailed out.

The Hurricane's advances served it well in the Battle of Britain, where the aircraft was assigned to more units and scored more victories than the more famous Supermarine Spitfire. Production ended in 1944, and most Hurricanes were replaced by more modern aircraft soon after World War II ended.

THE LAST OF THE MANY, THE FINAL HAWKER HURRICANE PRODUCED, LEFT THE FACTORY IN SEPTEMBER 1944.

BRITISH CAMOUFLAGE AND AMERICAN MARKINGS IDENTIFY THIS AS ONE OF THE P-40E-1S
BUILT FOR THE ROYAL AIR FORCE BUT PRESSED INTO AMERICAN SERVICE.

CURTISS P-40E-1 WARHAWK/ KITTYHAWK MARK IA

When the United States entered World War II in December 1941, its forces were woefully unprepared. The principal Army fighter, the Curtiss P-40 Warhawk, performed poorly at high altitudes. At lower altitudes, the aircraft flew well against European adversaries but could not match Japan's highly maneuverable fighters in a dogfight. By capitalizing on the P-40's advantages—high diving speed, heavy armament and armor, rugged construction—U.S. Army and Allied commanders would eventually hold the line against Japanese and German aggression until a new generation of American fighters could join the battle. Even then, Warhawks continued to serve in frontline units well into 1944.

The P-40E variant, which first entered service early in 1941, introduced a battery of six .50-caliber machine guns that exceeded the firepower of both European and Asian contemporaries. Curtiss produced 820 P-40Es for the U.S. Army Air Forces, as well as 1,500 similar P-40E-1s for Great Britain using Lend-Lease funds. In British service, these aircraft were designated the Kittyhawk Mark IA.

In most respects the cockpits of the P-40E and the P-40E-1 were identical. The instrument panel grouped flight instruments around the center of the panel, rather than organizing them in the British Basic Six arrangement. The cutout at the top of the panel held a U.S. N-3 gun sight, the standard reflecting gun sight for all early-War U.S. Army fighters and twin-engined bombers. The cylindrical fluorescent light on a flexible gray cable projecting from the base of the panel could be positioned to illuminate dials and switches for night flying. Most switches and controls were conveniently at hand, though the landing gear and flap levers were located uncomfortably below the pilot's left shoulder. In fact, pilots were cautioned not to confuse the two levers when taxiing as a mistake when trying to raise flaps could lead to expensive repairs.

The differences in the two cockpits reflected British practices. The factory generally substituted a formed Bakelite seat and British-supplied Sutton harnesses for the American aluminum seat and safety belts. British aircraft also carried additional radios beneath the right canopy rail as well as a British constant-flow oxygen regulator. These small differences had little effect on American pilots when several hundred P-40E-1s built for Britain's Royal Air Force were diverted to U.S. squadrons in the early days of the war.

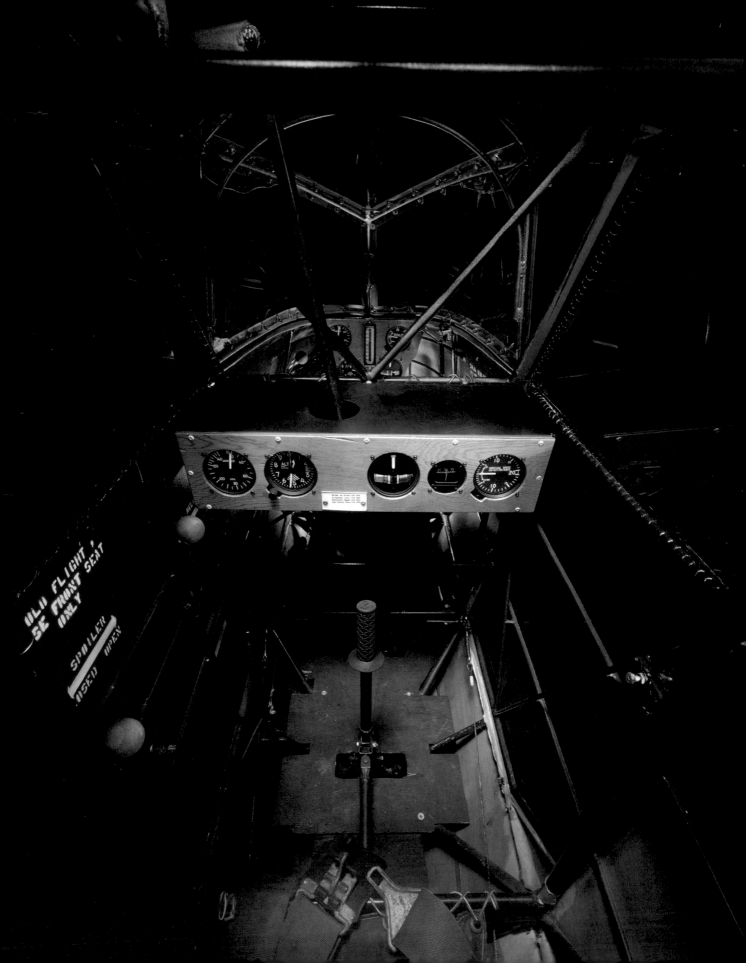

THE U.S. ARMY'S FIRST TRAINING GLIDER, THE FRANKFORT TG-1.

FRANKFORT TG-1A

Decades before the first powered airplane, gliders had been used for experimentation. But in May 1940, nine German gliders delivered combat troops to Belgian fort Eben-Emael, which was defending the Albert Canal; the so-called impregnable fortress fell within a few hours, and the attack ushered in a new form of warfare.

U.S. military planners moved to develop their own large combat gliders, as well as two-place gliders to train new glider pilots. The first of these training gliders was the TG-1, designed by Stan Corcoran of the Frankfort Sailplane Company. Essentially, Corcoran stretched his prewar Cinema I single-place glider to create an elongated cockpit with a second seat for the student. Frankfort produced a total of 43 TG-1s.

The TG-1 student and instructor sat tandem on canvas seats. Each had a control stick and rudder pedals, with simple instrument panels comprising air-speed indicators, altimeters, rate-of-climb indicators, turn and bank indicators, and compasses. The front seat, from which all solo flights were made, had an angle of attack indicator and provisions for a radio.

Once towed to altitude, either pilot could release the craft from the tow plane by pulling a wooden ball at the left of the instrument panel. Farther aft, a similar ball controlled the wing spoilers, which slowed forward motion and increased the rate of descent. The final control was a red-handled lever used to brake the single landing wheel on the ground.

THIS WARTIME PHOTO SHOWS AN F4U-1D

CARRYING TWO 500-POUND BOMBS.

STINSON L-5 SENTINEL

In the early days of World War II, European forces quickly learned that light attack and observation aircraft such as the Lysander could not survive in modern air combat. The U.S. Army knew that its own observation aircraft were not capable of spotting for their artillery. Paradoxically, while observation aircraft were too lightly armed and slow for the mission, unarmed aircraft, which were even slower, were perfect.

The foremost of these new light plane spotters were based on the civil Piper J-3 Cub and the Stinson Model 105 Voyager. Initially designated in the Army's observation series, they became, respectively, the O-59 and the O-62. In 1942, they were redesignated as liaison aircraft, becoming the L-4 Grasshopper and the L-5 Sentinel. Flying out of unimproved fields in every theater of war, they spotted artillery, evacuated the wounded, delivered supplies and personnel, and opened lines of communication.

The L-5 cockpit had no floor; the pilot sat over the fuselage framework and fabric skin, with foot channels leading to the rudder pedals. The throttle quadrant and trim tab control were above the left knee, with a flap control lever just aft. In many Sentinels, the observer had a duplicate set of controls, including a removable stick, in the backseat for pilot relief or training purposes.

The instrument panel carried a four-dial blind-flying arrangement (distinguished by a yellow border) and a few engine instruments. As on most early L-5s (this being the first one built), the electrical switches were to the left of the main panel. On later aircraft, the switches were moved to a separate overhead panel. Most radio equipment was controlled by the observer.

MARTIN B-26B
MARAUDER "FLAK BAIT"

The aircraft Martin B-26 Marauder was branded a "widow maker" by many crews, yet at the end of World War II the AAF had lost fewer Marauders than any other bomber. One Marauder nicknamed *Flak Bait* completed the war with 207 operational missions over Europe, more than any other American aircraft.

Early short-wing Marauders, designed for speed (323 mph), were often too hot for newly trained pilots. Single-engine performance was poor, landing and take-off speeds were high, and the aircraft was unforgiving of mistakes. Combined with engine and propeller malfunctions, excessive antiaircraft damage on low-altitude missions would initially cost the AAF many B-26s and their crews. Wing and tail surfaces were enlarged and that helped, as did an Army Air Forces decision to fly most missions above 10,000 feet.

The Marauder's five-man crew understood the meaning of "task saturation" long before the term became popular. The pilot did most of the flying, with a copilot and autopilot for relief on long flights. The copilot doubled as the navigator, spending much of his time in the compartment behind the flight deck (see detail on page 65). He shared this compartment with the radio operator, who was also required to man the dorsal turret and ventral guns. The bombardier, located in a compartment just forward of the flight deck, also manned the defensive nose guns. The final crewman, seated all the way aft, was the tail gunner.

Most instruments and controls were arranged around the pilot, with the copilot sharing all but the basic flight controls. Many switches, including the critical propeller feathering switches, were mounted on the top of the center pedestal, where throttles and other levers could block access in an emergency.

THIS EARLY B-26B SHOWS THE CLEAN LINES OF A DESIGN CREATED FOR SPEED.

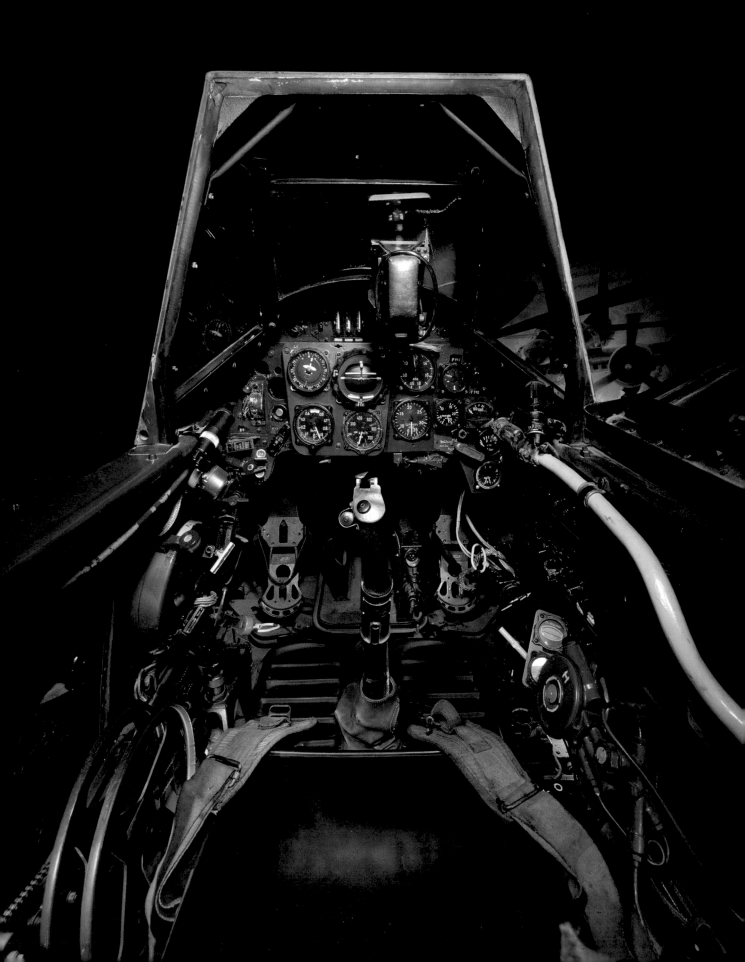

CAPTURED IN ITALY IN 1944, THIS BF 109 G-6 WAS EVALUATED BY THE U.S. ARMY AIR FORCES AT WRIGHT FIELD. IT WOULD BE RESTORED BY THE NATIONAL AIR AND SPACE MUSEUM THIRTY YEARS LATER.

MESSERSCHMITT BF 109 G-6

The Messerschmitt Bf 109 was the German Luftwaffe's principal offensive fighter of World War II. Tested in the Spanish Civil War and proven in the early assaults on Western Europe, the 109 fought wherever Germany invaded. Ultimately, it was overwhelmed as the Allies achieved aerial supremacy in the skies over Germany.

Designed by Professor Willy Messerschmitt in 1935, the Bf 109 was initially manufactured by the Bayerische Flugzeugwerke (Bavarian Flying Works) as a small, single-engine monoplane fighter with fully enclosed cockpit and retractable landing gear. Early combat versions carried two synchronized rifle-caliber machine guns that fired through the propeller arc, with provisions for a third that fired through the hub.

By late 1942, when the Bf 109 G-6 first appeared, the Messerschmitt fighter had progressed through many changes in power plant, armament, defensive armor, and aerodynamics, with commensurate increases in weight. The G-6, which carried two heavy machine guns and a centerline 20mm or 30mm cannon (with provisions for two underwing 20mm cannons), would be produced in greater numbers than any other 109 variant.

Although many aircraft in the G-series had pressurized cockpits, the G-6 did not. There was little room to spare in the cramped cockpit, but most controls were placed within the pilot's easy reach. The seat rested above the main fuel tank, with a yellow fuel line leading to the engine along the right canopy rail. (A clear plastic section in the line reassured the pilot the fuel was continuing to flow.) The instrument panel carried the blind-flying instruments at the center, with engine gauges to the right. Atop the panel was the standard German Revi gun sight, and below the panel (between the rudder pedals) was the butt of the heavy 30mm cannon. To the left of the seat, a large wheel allowed the pilot to crank down the landing gear in the event of a hydraulic failure.

LOCKHEED P-38J LIGHTNING

The Lockheed P-38 Lightning was the U.S. Army's most capable fighter during the first two years of World War II. One of the few successful twin-engined fighters of the day, the Lightning often enjoyed an advantage in speed, fire power, and maneuverability over its single-engined opponents. Battle-damaged Lightnings could fly home on a single engine, saving many pilots from death, injury, or captivity.

The Lightning wasn't perfect. The aircraft's high speeds put it into flight regimes that few others had encountered. In a dive, airflow over the wings could approach the speed of sound, causing a loss of control—a problem solved partially by redesigning the tail and later by adding underwing dive brakes. Lightnings were expensive and complicated to produce (only about 10,000 would be built) and maintain. Fuel quality and pilot training and inexperience contributed to early disappointments in the P-38's

performance over Europe. Most of these difficulties, though, were eventually overcome.

The Lightning pilot sat in cramped quarters, often contending with the cold of higher altitudes; the prominent cockpit-heat lever to the right of the windscreen never adequately overcame the problem. The cockpit remained unpressurized on all Lightnings, increasing pilot fatigue and discomfort as flight levels approached 40,000 feet.

Using a novel control-stick arrangement, designers added to the small space provided for the pilot's legs. The main column was set to the right, then angled over to the center of the cockpit. The early rounded control wheel used to roll the aircraft was soon replaced by a twin-grip design.

An innovative console carried many switches below and ahead of the instrument panel, though access to the console was often blocked by the control column.

A FLIGHT OF BUBBLE-TOPPED P-47DS ON A STATESIDE TRAINING MISSION.

REPUBLIC P-47D-30 THUNDERBOLT

In size, weight, and armament, the P-47 Thunderbolt exceeded every other single-seat, single-engine fighter of World War II. By mating the Pratt & Whitney R-2800 engine (as used in the Vought F4U Corsair) with a General Electric supercharger, Republic Aviation created the first production Army fighter capable of speeds over 400 mph in level flight. With a battery of eight .50-caliber machine guns and an unequaled ability to survive heavy battle damage, the P-47 would excel at both air-to-air combat and ground attack. Built in greater quantities than any other American fighter, the Thunderbolt would remain in service with the Air National Guard until 1954.

This massive aircraft also offered the roomiest cockpit of its day. Beneath the cockpit floor, ducts connected the supercharger in the rear fuselage to the engine; in the event of a crash landing, these ducts also protected the pilot by absorbing much of the impact. In mid-1944, Republic improved all-around visibility with the introduction of a heavy, electrically operated bubble canopy. The arrangement of controls and instruments was orderly through the entire production run, and the few minor cockpit changes reflected the introduction of new equipment. A Mark 8 gun sight (similar to the Corsair's) was fitted to a cutout in the center of the instrument board. Below and to either side, the flight instruments were grouped within a white borderline.

The power plant was controlled by four levers at the pilot's right hand. The large throttle handle was capped by a smaller switch that injected water into the engine cylinders for short bursts of additional power, while the three smaller levers bore distinguishing letters: B for boost (supercharger), P for propeller pitch, and M for mixture. When the combination of weight and power brought diving speeds near the speed of sound, pilots were cautioned to open recovery flaps (with a red switch at the front of the left canopy rail) to decelerate and restore control.

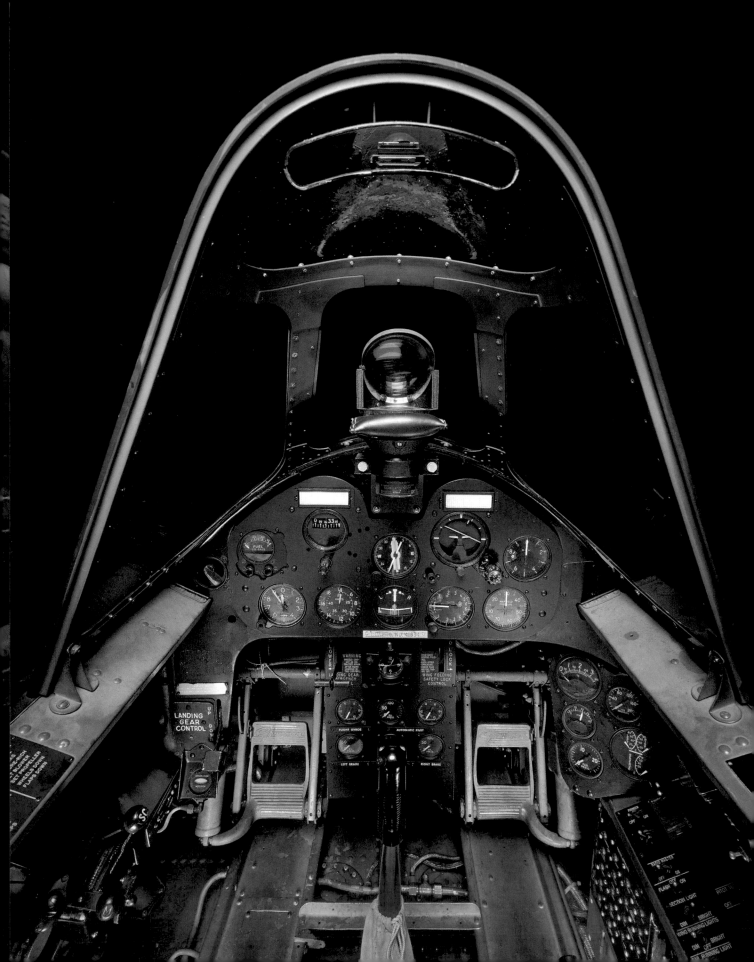

THE GRUMMAN F6F-3 HELLCAT WAS THE AIRCRAFT THAT GAVE THE U.S. NAVY

ITS FIRST PERFORMANCE ADVANTAGE OVER JAPANESE FIGHTERS.

GRUMMAN F6F-3 HELLCAT

Entering service in summer 1943, the Grumman F6F Hellcat was the first U.S. Navy carrier-based fighter with enough speed and maneuverability to wrest control of the skies from the Japanese. Although it did not complete its first combat mission until August 31, 1943, the Hellcat over the next two years would produce 305 aces (more than any other American aircraft) and destroy more than 55 percent of all enemy aircraft claimed by U.S. Navy and Marine pilots during the entire war.

Development of the F6F began in September 1940. The Navy ordered prototypes the next June and placed its first production order in January 1942, six months before the first flight. Production aircraft flew with a version of the same Pratt & Whitney R-2800 engine that powered the Corsair and the Thunderbolt.

The Hellcat was a large aircraft, and pilots found its cockpit roomy and comfortable. Instruments and controls were easily reachable and well organized,

an advantage to any pilot during either training or combat. Visibility was excellent, particularly during approaches for landings on aircraft carriers.

The Hellcat required less muscle to fly than the earlier F4F Wildcat. A single switch replaced the manual crank for raising and lowering landing gear. Another switch automatically folded or opened wings for storage aboard carriers.

About 1,700 Hellcats were modified as night fighters, with a short-range (3–4 miles) radar pod mounted on one wing and a radar scope centered on the instrument panel. At a time when most of the world's night fighters were twin-engined aircraft with a second crewman to operate the radar, Hellcat pilots were surprisingly effective against night intruders. Following World War II, most surviving Hellcats were moved to support and training roles, though operational night fighters were retained through mid-1954.

KAWASAKI KI-45 KAI HEI TORYU

Development of the heavy fighter, an aircraft packing large-caliber weapons and possessing exceptional speed and range, proved a popular undertaking for interwar air forces. Generally powered by two engines and seating two, a majority of these designs failed during development; most of the rest failed in their first encounters with the newer generation of single seat fighters. The remaining heavy fighters invariably found a niche as bomber destroyers, strike aircraft, or the first generation of night fighters. In the Japanese Army, these three roles would be filled by one heavy fighter, the Ki-45 (pronounced "key" 45).

Although design work for the Kawasaki Ki-45 began in early 1938, the aircraft had an abnormally long gestation period. The first prototypes were woefully underpowered; designers returned with new engines and a host of aerodynamic revisions. Production of this Ki-45 Kai (short for *Kaizo*, or "modified") was finally authorized in late 1941, and aircraft began reaching operational units in August 1942.

The type was called Toryu ("dragon killer") in Japan or Nick by the Allies. In 1943, a new night fighter variant was ordered into production as the Ki-45 Kai Hei (or Type C). Of the 1,700 Ki-45s built, 477 would be Type Kai Hei night fighters.

The Ki-45 Kai Hei cockpit was cramped, subject to excessive vibration, and poorly laid out. The artificial horizon, a critical instrument for any extended period of night flying, was hidden behind the control stick.

As a night fighter, the Toryu was designed to have a centimetric radar mounted in its nose, though this installation was never used operationally. Interceptions were therefore made visually, with basic guidance from ground radar controllers. If the pilot chose to attack from below, the top button on his control stick fired two 20mm cannon obliquely upward into the target's belly. For more conventional attacks, the button to the left fired a heavy 37mm cannon sighted along the Toryu's centerline.

TORYU, THE DRAGON KILLER, PROVED TO BE AN EFFECTIVE THREAT TO U.S. B-29 FORMATIONS OVER JAPAN.

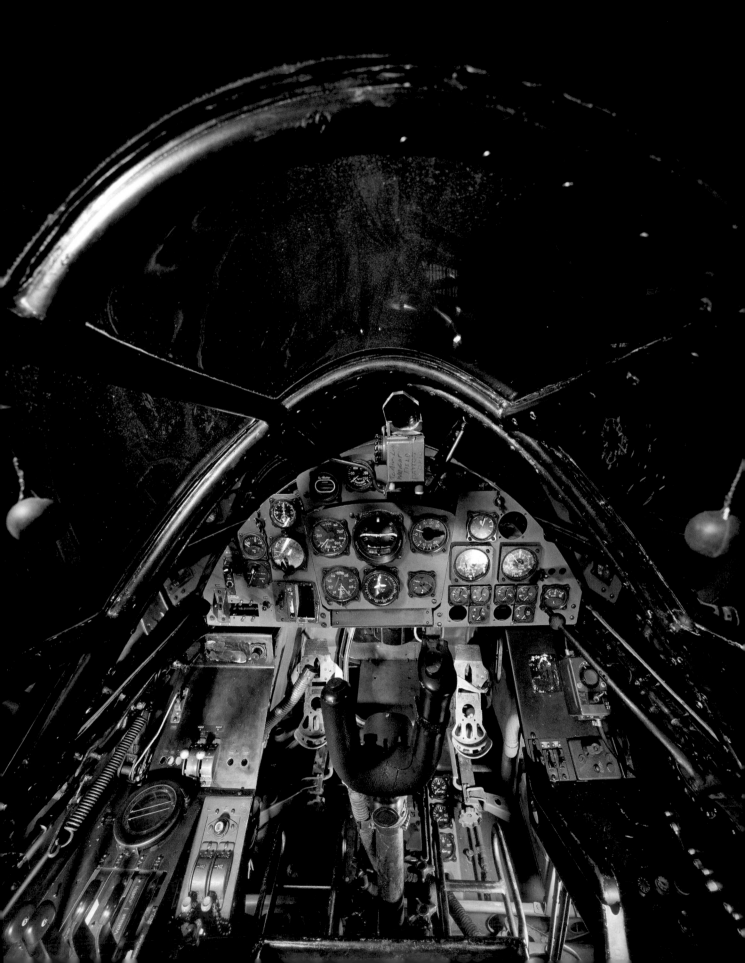

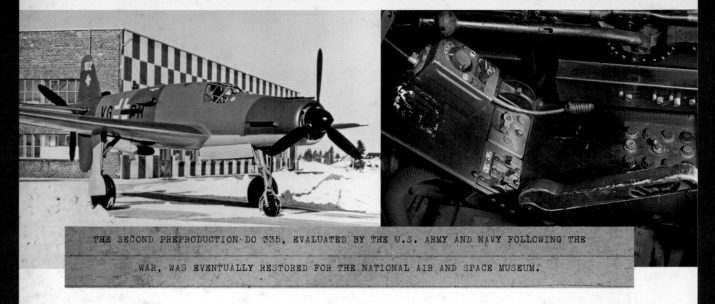

DORNIER DO 335 PFEIL

The Dornier Do 335 Pfeil (Arrow) was the fastest piston-engined fighter ever produced. An innovation in design allowed Dornier to place one powerful Daimler-Benz DB-603 engine in the nose, driving a three-blade tractor propeller, with a second DB-603 behind the pilot driving a pusher prop. The Do 335 was an exceptionally large and heavy, twin-engined, single-seat fighter with remarkable acceleration and turning radius.

The first developmental contract for Do 335 prototypes was let in January 1943; tests of the first prototype began that December. Further contracts ordered fighter, trainer, night fighter, reconnaissance and bomber variants of the Pfeil, but none would ever see combat. Allied strategic bombers were attacking Germany's industrial base, and they destroyed the factory and tooling for the Do 335 in early 1944. Factories building engines, components, and subassemblies were also targeted, as were the transportation networks needed to deliver those parts. By war's end, production

had been completed on only about 50 Do 335s (mostly prototype and developmental airframes), with another 85 aircraft found in various stages of completion at Dornier's ruined factories.

The cockpit of the Do 335 was unusually large and comfortable. The pilot sat on one of the world's first ejection seats, which reclined 13 degrees. In an emergency, three console buttons to the right of the instrument panel (see above, right) armed the ejection seat and fired explosive bolts to clear away the rear propeller and upper vertical tail. Two large levers at either side of the main panel then released the canopy, and compressed air would launch the seat and pilot from the doomed aircraft. The eleventh prototype successfully tested the rear-propeller explosive system, but no pilot ever used the Do 335's ejection seat.

A similar system allowed the pilot to blow off the ventral tail surfaces and aft propeller before a crash landing.

JUNKERS JU 388 L-1

During World War II, each nation was forced to weigh the performance advantages of new aircraft designs against the production advantages of improved older designs. For Germany in 1943, the choice was often complicated by increasing Allied attacks on the country's industry, raw materials, and transportation.

This is how Germany's most versatile aircraft, the Junkers Ju 88, was developed into the Ju 188 in 1942; three greatly improved Ju 188 variants were redesignated Ju 388 in 1943. The three high-altitude versions were designed for very different missions: the Ju 388 J (originally Ju 188 J) was a night fighter; the Ju 388 K (Ju 188 K), a bomber; and the Ju 388 L (Ju 188 L), a reconnaissance aircraft. In all, about 60 of the 80-some aircraft completed by war's end were reconnaissance variants, and few (if any) flew operationally.

The Ju 388's three-man crew crowded into the pressurized cockpit through a floor hatch. The radio operator/gunner/navigator sat behind the pilot, facing aft (see page 83). His equipment included a periscope linked to gun sights above and below the fuselage. A handle and small joy stick operated the remote tail turret, a stinger with two heavy machine guns mounted on it. Due to developmental difficulties with this turret, some Ju 388 Ls seated a fourth crewman beside the radio operator to fire a flexible machine gun, which was mounted in a cutout made in the rear canopy. This gunner held one end of his machine gun, and swiveled and fired to ward off fighters.

The pilot had excellent forward and downward vision, though the canopy's greenhouse framing restricted visibility in every other direction. Primary engine instruments and controls were situated to his left, with temperature, pressure, and fuel gauges, and wheel and flap controls easily within reach on the right. As with many other German combat aircraft, the throttles were designed to automatically select the correct propeller pitch and fuel mixture for any power setting. Flight instruments were suspended to the right. (The English annotations next to most instruments and controls were added by AAF evaluators when the aircraft was tested at Wright Field after the war.)

The observer was last to enter. His seat, stowed behind the pilot's seat, swung out and down to its flight position, which was to the right of and behind the pilot.

The cockpit air-conditioning system was inadequate for the temperatures experienced in the Ju 388 cockpit. On the ground, crewmen learned the true meaning of the greenhouse effect, with fixed windows that didn't open to vent the heat. At high altitudes, frigid temperatures were relieved by the crew's electrically heated flight suits, each controlled by its own plug-in box and controls.

THIS JU 388 L WAS TESTED AT WRIGHT FIELD AFTER THE WAR. THE LONG GONDOLA

BENEATH THE FUSELAGE HOUSED RECONNAISSANCE CAMERAS.

FOLLOWING THE WAR, THE FRENCH, BRITISH, SOVIETS, CZECHS, AND AMERICANS EVALUATED THE

CAPTURED HE 219S. THIS WAS ONE OF FOUR EVALUATED BY THE ROYAL AIR FORCE.

HEINKEL HE 219 UHU

Germany's finest night fighter, the Heinkel He 219 Uhu (Eagle Owl) entered combat on the night of June 11–12, 1943. A single preproduction He 219 A-0 based at Venlo, Netherlands, slipped into the British bomber stream and destroyed five four-engined bombers in a half hour.

Designed in mid-1940 as a multirole fighter, the He 219 found little support in the German Air Ministry (RLM). Germany expected to win the war soon using improved versions of existing aircraft and, more importantly, company head Ernst Heinkel had political enemies in the Ministry.

The increasing pressure of the British Royal Air Force's night bombing campaign forced the RLM to rethink its decision. The German night fighter force, comprising heavy day fighters and converted high-speed bombers, was too slow. At the end of 1941,

Heinkel was directed to convert his design into a radar-equipped night fighter; in November 1942, the first prototype took to the air, and soon after, 300 production aircraft were ordered.

Production would not come easy, despite the Uhu's popularity and success with the night fighter force. The combination of Allied bomber attacks on Heinkel factories and RLM antagonism meant that only 294 He 219s were completed.

The He 219 crew operated as part of an integrated night fighter force. With RAF night bombers attacking in streams of individual aircraft, rather than large formations, Luftwaffe ground controllers vectored each fighter to a separate target. The radar operator took over once the short-range, onboard radar detected the enemy, and he directed his pilot until the foe could be identified and attacked visually.

The two-man crew sat back-to-back in a pressurized cockpit beneath a clear canopy with fewer frames than usual for a German aircraft. Ultraviolet lighting illuminated the flight instruments without damaging night vision (see below, left). Each crewman had a long red handle to fire his compressed-air ejection seat; the crew of one Uhu would be saved by history's first combat ejection on the night of April 11, 1944.

The aft fuselage of the A-2 variant included an unpressurized compartment for a third crewman (see below right). Seated on webbing strung between fuselage formers, this technician could fine-tune the radar sets or help train operators. Many He 219s would use this compartment to mount the Schrage Musik (Jazz Music) obliquely firing cannon, an installation first pioneered on the Kawasaki Ki-45.

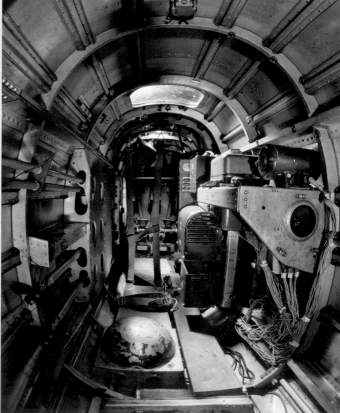

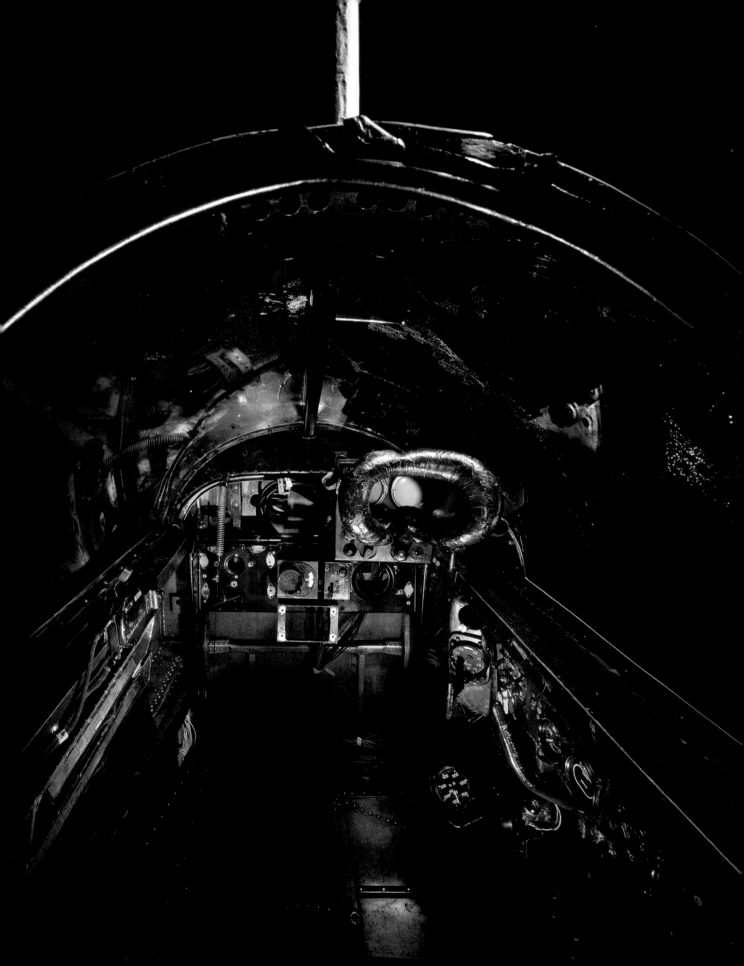

DIFFICULTIES WITH THE XP-80'S HALFORD ENGINE LED TO THE USE OF THE

GENERAL ELECTRIC I-40/J33 IN ALL SUBSEQUENT AIRCRAFT.

LOCKHEED XP-80
SHOOTING STAR "LULU-BELLE"

America's first operational jet aircraft, the Lockheed P-80 (or F-80, after June 1948) Shooting Star, emerged too late to see combat in World War II. But in November 1950, it was a Shooting Star that met a MiG-15 in the skies over Korea for the world's first jet-vs.-jet combat. Re-engined and equipped with radar and rockets, the F-80 became the F-94, the United States' first all-weather jet interceptor. Equipped with dual controls, the F-80 developed into the T-33, one of the Free World's first great jet trainers.

At the beginning of World War II, Germany and Great Britain led the world in jet engine development. Germany flew its first jet aircraft in 1939. The first British jet aircraft, which flew in May 1941, was still in ground tests when Army Air Forces Commanding General H.H. Arnold visited in April. Britain acceded to Arnold's request for information, providing the engines, drawings, and test data needed to jump-start America's jet program.

The Bell XP-59 came first. Ordered in September 1941, the twin-engined jet first flew one year later. Useful as a developmental aircraft, the XP-59 would not perform well enough for combat. In June 1943, the AAF asked Lockheed to design a fighter powered by the British Halford H-1B Goblin jet engine. The resulting XP-80, nicknamed *Lulu-Belle*, first flew on January 8, 1944. At a time when piston-engined fighters were struggling with speeds in the 400 mph range, *Lulu-Belle* reached 547 mph.

Pilots found the XP-80 surprisingly quiet and free of vibration. *Lulu-Belle*'s unpressurized cockpit was generally spacious, though leg room was limited by the two machine guns mounted beneath the floor. (At a time when most prototypes were unarmed, *Lulu-Belle* carried six .50-caliber machine guns in the nose.)

Early jet engines were sensitive to adjustments, as the placard beneath the throttle warned. Rapid throttle movement often caused a flameout, occasionally with fatal results.

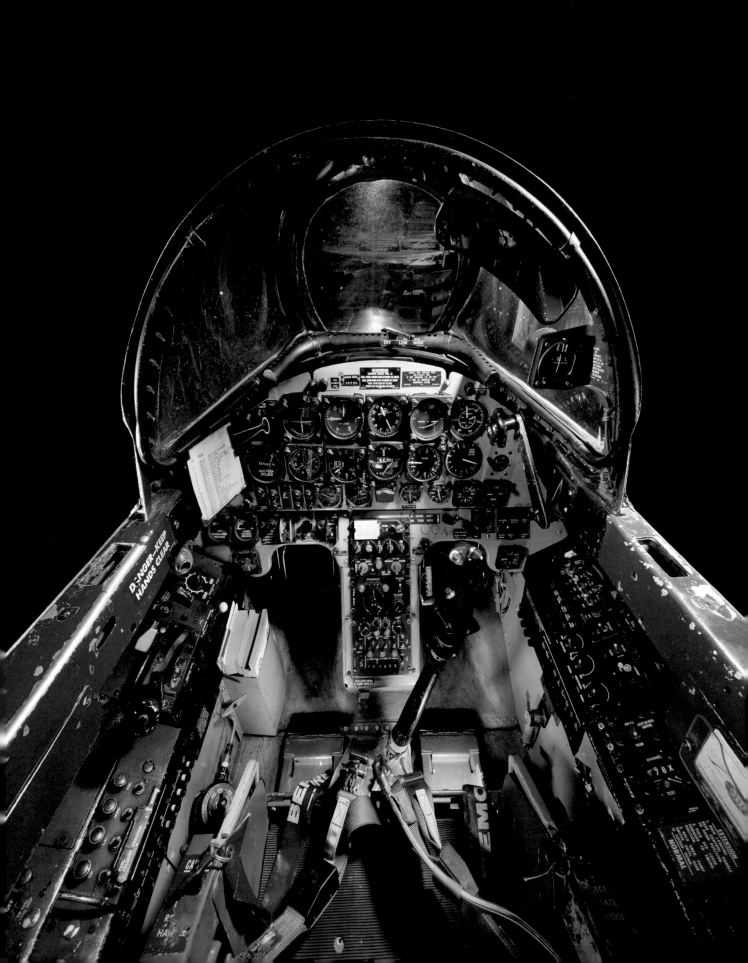

LOCKHEED T-33A SHOOTING STAR

After World War II, the United States Air Force began converting to jets and training the pilots to fly them. "Every man a tiger" was the slogan, and the aircraft that helped thousands become tigers was the T-33.

By 1947, the need for a jet trainer became critical. P-80s had been in more than 60 accidents, most due to pilots' unfamiliarity with jet idiosyncracies. Lockheed stretched a P-80C, adding an instructor's seat behind the pilot. The second seat reduced fuselage fuel capacity, but Lockheed compensated by adding two large, wingtip fuel tanks.

The first flight of the TP-80 was in March 1948. The aircraft was redesignated TF-80 that June, and T-33 in May 1949. But to her pilots, this aircraft would forever be known as the T-Bird. Through the late 1950s, most U.S. military pilots would learn about jets in a T-Bird. Over 6,500 were built, including those produced in Canada and Japan. The last T-33 left USAF service in 1987.

Those fortunate enough to fly in the T-33, whether student pilots, instructors, passengers, or even ROTC students who earned an "incentive flight," remember the cockpit as close but comfortable. In decent weather, the hydraulic canopy was left open until just before takeoff; bright red paint on either side served as a reminder that the canopy rail was not designed as an armrest. In an emergency, a yellow handle to the left of the right rudder pedal jettisoned the canopy. Raising the yellow handles at either thigh armed the seat, and squeezing the trigger inside the handle launched the seat and its occupant clear of the aircraft. Those unclear of the procedure had little worry—controls in the rear allowed the instructor to eject both seats.

In the 1950s, a series of T-33 accidents was eventually traced to the placement of the IFF (identification, friend or foe) panel at the console base between the pilot's knees. Instructed by ground controllers to "squawk" the transponder (press the button that identifies your aircraft to our radar), pilots would often move the control stick slightly, lean forward, and activate the signal. With the aircraft at high speed and turning slightly, the pilot's equilibrium would be disturbed as he sat up, and vertigo would result. Totally disoriented, some pilots flew into the ground before they could regain their balance. To this day, the USAF uses a T-33 simulator to train pilots how to react to vertigo.

MANY T-33S SERVED AS "BANDITS," ATTEMPTING TO ENTER NORTH
AMERICAN AIRSPACE WHILE EVADING DEFENSIVE FIGHTERS.
THE T-BIRD'S STEALTHY DESIGN WAS TRACKED MORE EASILY
WHEN A TRAVEL POD WAS MOUNTED UNDER THE AFT FUSELAGE.

NORTH AMERICAN FJ-1 FURY

One of the U.S. Navy's first jets, the North American FJ-1 Fury was quickly overshadowed by newer designs. First flown in September 1946, the last FJ-1 would be transferred to the Naval Air Reserve in May 1949, after only 14 months of operational service. The last three aircraft would be stricken from the Reserve lists in 1954. Although only 33 were built (including three prototypes), the FJ-1 would sire the West's first line of great jet fighters. Redesigned with swept-back wings and a stretched fuselage, the aircraft became the Air Force's F-86 Sabre and the Navy's FJ-2, FJ-3, and FJ-4 Furies.

North American Aviation and the Navy took a conservative approach to designing the FJ-1, retaining simple, proven systems and configurations whenever possible. The thin, straight laminar flow wing did not fold, and there were no underwing hard points for external stores. Wingtip fuel tanks of 165 gallons each were a necessity for flights of any duration.

Tricycle landing gear prevented the jet efflux from tearing up carrier decks and runways, but the nose gear proved too weak for the stress of carrier landings. Six .50-caliber machine guns were mounted in the nose, three on either side of the jet intake.

FJ-1 pilots flew from a conventional seat beneath a sliding bubble canopy. To improve visibility during landing and takeoff, most pilots opened the canopy and, using a floor-mounted handle at the left hip, raised the seat. The unpressurized cockpit included fresh air vents, but pilots complained of the poor heating and cooling.

The instrument panel was divided by a sliding chart board; all naval aviators were expected to navigate their aircraft to and from carriers without benefit of landmarks. Flight instruments were centered on the panel, above and below the board, with a Mark 23 computing gun sight at the top. A hydraulic boost system helped decrease stick forces, reducing pilot fatigue.

THE THREE AIRCRAFT MARKETED BY PIPER FROM 1955 TO 1957 WERE (FRONT TO REAR): THE PA-18 SUPER CUB, THE PA-22 TRIPACER, AND THE PA-23 APACHE.

PIPER PA-18 SUPER CUB

The last of the Piper Cubs, the PA-18 Super Cub was introduced in November 1949 and remained in continuous production until 1982. Piper reintroduced the design in 1988 and continued building Super Cubs until 1994; the type is still produced by a number of companies, often in kit form. Piper produced some 10,300 PA-18s, including 1,800 for U.S. and foreign armed forces.

This particular PA-18 was one of several operated by the U.S. Atomic Energy Commission (AEC) in the mid-1950s. Equipped with "scintillation" measurement and recording equipment, the aircraft surveyed the western United States to help locate radioactive uranium deposits for America's growing nuclear industry. The Super Cub proved perfect for the job: inexpensive to purchase, maintain, and fly; slow and stable enough for the sensitive onboard instruments; and dependable at extremely low altitudes above sparsely populated, inhospitable terrain.

Working in and over the wilderness, each of the AEC's Super Cub pilots was rated as a commercial pilot as well as being a licensed airframe and power plant (A&E) mechanic. Similarly, each geologist/ observer had sufficient training to pilot the airplane in an emergency. With the fuel tank mounted in the root of the left wing, the Super Cub had a different center of gravity than the original J-3 Cub. The pilot now flew from the front seat, even on solo flights. Opposite the fuel tank, a generator panel occupied the root of the right-wing.

The instrument panel carried six flight instruments, three engine instruments, and a switch for the electric starter. Centered beneath the panel was a Narco Superhomer radio, complete with navigation receiver. Following World War II, the U.S. began installing medium-range radio transmitters at stations around the country. The system was known as the very high frequency omni-directional radio range or VOR (sometimes also called the VHF omni range, or omni). This early, pre-transistor Superhomer, with tubes and crystals to receive only four frequencies, combined a communications radio and a navigation radio into a single set as one of the first NAV/COM systems available for civil aviation.

TODAY, SCOTTY MCCRAY'S 2-22EK IS DISPLAYED AT

THE NATIONAL AIR AND SPACE MUSEUM'S STEVEN F. UDVAR-HAZY CENTER.

SCHWEIZER SGU 2-22EK

Anticipating a post-World War II resurgence in private flying, in late 1945 brothers Earnest, Paul, and William Schweizer designed a rugged, stable utility glider that would appeal to flight schools, flying clubs, and private owners. The SGU 2-22 (Schweizer Glider, Utility type, two-seat, Model 22) featured a fabric-covered, chrome-molybdenum steel tube fuselage. The aluminum-frame wing had aluminum skin for the first third of the chord, with fabric covering the remainder.

The first flight occured in 1946, but early sales were disappointing in a market flooded with war-surplus training gliders. Schweizer production averaged fewer than five 2-22s per year through 1957. In 1963, the company introduced the SGU 2-22E with a new molded canopy, increased upward visibility in the aft seat, longer wing spoilers, and small wingtip wheels for smoother, unassisted takeoffs and easier ground handling; it was also available in kit form as the 2-22EK. When the last 2-22 was delivered in 1967, Schweizer had produced a total of 258 aircraft and kits.

Early 2-22s left the rear cockpit open; the instructor simply leaned out of either side to see ahead.

Later models raised the rear seat and improved canopy glazing to offer better forward visibility from inside the cockpit. Solo flights were made from the front seat.

The standard instrument panel came with an airspeed indicator and a red knob to release the tow able. (The instructor's release knob was mounted in the back of the student's seat.) The lever at the left opened the overwing spoilers, springing shut automatically when released. The same lever, when pulled through its last half inch of travel, activated the wheel brake. A two-position lever on the floor beneath the panel trimmed the aircraft; the forward setting was used during towing and solo flight, and the aft was used when both seats were occupied.

The late Byron G. "Scotty" McCray demonstrated the SGU 2-22EK at air shows throughout the U.S., Canada, and the Bahamas between 1966 and 1973. Considered the Master of Unpowered Flight, McCray synchronized each performance to music broadcast over public address systems. His upgraded instrument panel included an altimeter, compass, accelerometer, and radio.

ART SCHOLL'S MODIFIED CHIPMUNK PENNZOIL SPECIAL,

DISPLAYED AT THE STEVEN F. UDVAR-HAZY CENTER.

DE HAVILLAND-CANADA DHC-1A CHIPMUNK "PENNZOIL SPECIAL"

De Havilland Aircraft of Canada, Ltd., was established in 1928 to assemble aircraft shipped as components from their parent company in the U.K. The company began wholesale manufacture of many de Havilland models shortly before World War II and built the first aircraft of its own design in 1946. The DHC-1 Chipmunk was a two-place monoplane *ab initio* trainer that served Canadian, British, Commonwealth, and Allied military pilots before being sold as surplus to the civilian market in the late 1950s and early 1960s.

Veteran aerobatic and movie pilot Art Scholl purchased two of the Chipmunks, one of which he modified dramatically in the late 1960s. Scholl, a pilot holding every U.S. rating—licensed airframe and power plant (A&P) mechanic, aeronautical engineer, university professor, three-time member of the U.S. Aerobatic Team, FAA Inspector, and fixed-base operator with a school of international aerobatics—brought a host of qualifications to the project. His *Pennzoil Special* was

now a single-seat aerobatic aircraft with retractable landing gear, a 260-horsepower Lycoming engine, and tanks to mark Scholl's aerobatic routines with red, white, and blue smoke trails. Scholl skillfully demonstrated the modified Chipmunk's capabilities throughout North America until his death in 1985.

The *Pennzoil Special's* cockpit was completely upgraded to meet Scholl's needs as both an aerobatic and cross-country flyer. The control stick was extended by 3 inches to ease the loads of his more severe aerobatic routines. The flap lever and the underwing landing flaps were removed to lengthen the ailerons and save weight. The cockpit clock was replaced by a stopwatch, an improvement for the split-second timing of aerobatic routines, and an accelerometer was added to measure stresses on airframe and pilot. The base of the panel held a sophisticated Bendix NAV/COMM radio, DME (distance-measuring equipment), and an instrument landing system Course Deviation Indicator.

MIKOYAN-GURYEVICH MIG-15BIS (J-2)

In October 1950, the Korean War seemed near an end. Communist North Korea's invasion of South Korea the previous June was countered by the United Nations, which established air superiority, invaded, and quickly reoccupied most of the Korean Peninsula. Then, on November 1, Communist Chinese forces attacked with six vastly superior, Russian-built Mikoyan-Guryevich MiG-15 fighters. A new phase of the air battle had begun, and Chinese ground troops soon joined the land battle; the Korean War would last until July 1953.

Western observers had been aware of the new fighter, but its performance came as a shock. The U.S. brought in North American F-86s, which equaled the MiG-15's performance, but superior training more than any technological advantage was responsible for the U.N. reclaiming the skies.

The MiG was designed in 1946 at a time when Soviet premier Joseph Stalin was desperate to maintain military parity with the West. Lagging behind in jet development, the Soviets simply requested help from the British, who were pleased to share the latest Rolls Royce Nene and Derwent engines. Copied and refined, these engines were married to a design under way at the Mikoyan and Guryevich design bureau. The clean, lightweight fighter featured tricycle landing gear and, for the first time in Soviet engineering, a radically swept-back wing, a pressurized cockpit, and an ejection seat.

More than 16,000 MiG-15s were produced, including 800 two-seat trainers built in China. MiG-15 fighters in Chinese service, all of Soviet manufacture, were designated Jianji 2 or J-2 (often anglicized as Fighter 2 or F-2). The improved MiG-15*bis* (or second variant) was also supplied to China, though sources dispute whether the type was designated J-2 or J-4.

The MiG-15*bis* had excellent pressurization; pilots could fly at 30,000 feet without use of their oxygen masks. In 1952, a g-suit system was added to aircraft on production lines. Thus equipped, pilots stood a better chance of avoiding blackouts during combat maneuvers. A number of MiG-15s were equipped with a rudimentary Soviet instrument landing system, though this equipment was not installed on aircraft built for export.

SHORTLY AFTER THE KOREAN WAR, A NORTH KOREAN PILOT DEFECTED TO THE WEST WITH THIS MIG-15BIS, GIVING UNITED NATIONS FORCES THEIR FIRST CHANCE TO EXAMINE THE AIRCRAFT IN DETAIL.

BOEING 367-80

The father of the first generation of American jet transports, the Boeing 367-80 (or, Dash 80) prototype made its first flight on July 15, 1954. Adaptations of this basic design would become the revolutionary 707 and 720 series of civil jet airliners, the KC-135 line of military tankers and transports, and the E-3, E-6, and E-8 family of electronic warning and control aircraft. The single Dash 80 prototype continued to serve Boeing as a flying test bed until retiring in 1972.

The concept began as a Boeing attempt to build a jet version of its military model 367 (KC-97), a straight-winged, piston-engined tanker. With no military or civil backing, Boeing invested $16 million of its own capital in the venture, an investment that paid off handsomely with eventual production of more than 1,000 707s and more than 700 military KC-135s. The success of the series established Boeing as a world leader in commercial jet transportation; more than a half century later, that success has translated into 14,000-plus orders for Boeing jet airliners.

The 367-80 was crewed by two pilots and a flight engineer, though other engineers or technicians were often accommodated up in the cockpit or fuselage. The austere cockpit was designed for airframe and power plant test and evaluation, with crew comfort of secondary importance. Instruments and controls could be added or replaced as necessary, particularly with new engines. (The Dash 80 once flew with three different types of jet engines beneath the wings, and, in another series of tests, with a fifth jet mounted on the aft fuselage.)

Flight tests, which might last for hours, generally orbited a test range rather than covering long stretches of territory; as might be expected, the main panel carried minimal navigational instrumentation. There is an inconsistent arrangement of pilot and copilot flight instruments, suggesting modifications at different times in the test program.

KNOWN AS THE CRANBERRY TO ITS CREWS, THE B-57 WAS A CLASSIC DESIGN OF THE COLD-WAR ERA.

THE EB-57A, SEEN HERE, FLEW WITH THE SAME FISH-BOWL CANOPY AS THE EARLY BRITISH CANBERRAS.

MARTIN EB-57B CANBERRA

Designed for the Royal Air Force as a high-altitude medium bomber, the English Electric Canberra is one of a small number of British combat aircraft to be produced under license in the United States. In 1950, the U.S. Air Force had a well-established strategic heavy bomber program, but its tactical jet bomber designs were failing to perform as expected. Demonstrations of the Canberra, which had first flown in 1949, showed an aircraft with high-subsonic speed, high ceiling, and moderate internal-bomb capacity of just over 3 tons. The RAF ferried a Canberra demonstrator to the U.S. in February 1951—making this the first jet crossing of the Atlantic—and a month later, the Glenn L. Martin Company was contracted to initiate production, integrating American engines and systems. The first American Canberra, designated B-57A, took to the skies on July 20, 1953. Martin produced a total of 403 B-57s, ending production in 1959.

The original B-57A featured the same fixed, fish-bowl canopy carried on early British Canberras.

The crew entered through a hatch beneath the fuselage, with the pilot sitting at the left side of the fuselage, beneath the canopy. The navigator sat farther aft and to the right, but within the fuselage, not under the canopy. There was a crawlway forward to operate equipment in the nose compartment.

After the 75th A-model, Martin introduced the B-57B, with tandem seating beneath a traditional clamshell canopy. At the end of their careers, a number of B-57Bs were converted to electronic-countermeasures platforms. Designated EB-57Bs, these aircraft were configured to test North America's air defenses, jamming ground-based radars and evading interceptors.

The B-57B cockpit was a tighter fit than crews had found in the more open B-57A. The forward crew compartment and crawlway were eliminated, but now, both crew members sat under the canopy. Perhaps it was a sign of the times that each crewman had an ashtray mounted within easy reach.

McDonnell F4H-1 (F-4A) Phantom II "Sageburner"

Designed for the U.S. Navy as a high-speed, carrier-borne interceptor, the McDonnell F4H-1 Phantom II made its first flight on May 27, 1958. By 1962, it would break most of the world's speed and altitude records. In March of that year, the U.S. Air Force would break tradition, ordering its own Phantom II, designated as the F-110. It was intended for close air support, interdiction, and air defense, making this the first ever Air Force order for a Navy fighter.

In October 1962, the Air Force and Navy adopted a common designation system, and the Phantom II became the F-4; early Navy aircraft were redesignated F-4A and F-4B, and the first USAF aircraft became F-4Cs. Production ended in 1981, after more than 5,000 Phantom IIs had been delivered to the military forces of the United States, the United Kingdom, Israel, Germany, Japan, Iran, and Turkey.

Sageburner, the second Phantom II of that name, was one of the first record-breaking Navy F4Hs.

On August 28, 1961, Lts. Huntington Hardisty (pilot) and Earl H. DeEsch set a world low-altitude speed record on a 3-km course. Flying at 125 feet above the desert floor, they averaged 902.769 mph, a record that stands to this day.

Seated in tandem, the F4H's two-man crew was trained to operate their aircraft as a missile platform. The pilot flew the aircraft and launched heat-seeking Sidewinder missiles at targets. In the rear seat, the RIO (Radar Intercept Officer, also called GIB or Guy in Back) tracked targets and directed the radar-guided Sparrow missiles. As a team, the crew shared credits for aerial victories scored during the Vietnam War.

As the eighth Phantom II built, *Sageburner* was considered a developmental airframe. But a quick comparison with the pilot's cockpit of an F-4S (see page 110), one of the last Marine Corps Phantoms to retire (in 1988), shows how little the layout changed over three decades.

THE SIXTH PHANTOM II RIDES THE ELEVATOR FROM

THE HANGAR DECK DURING CARRIER QUALIFICATION

TESTS ON BOARD THE U.S.S. INTREPID.

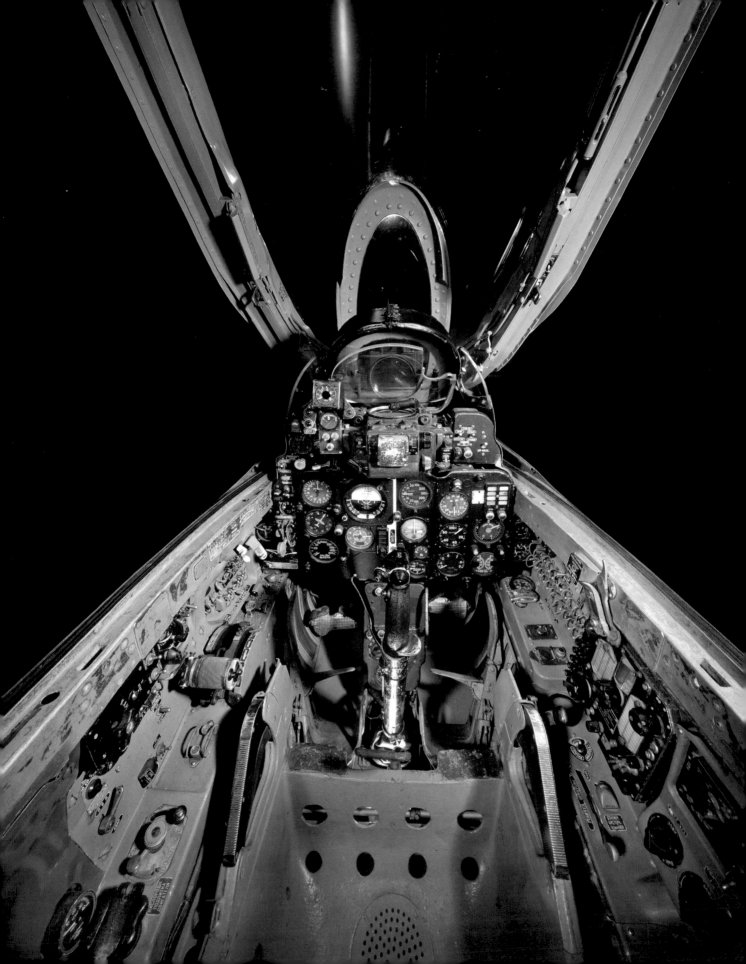

MIKOYAN-GURYEVICH MIG-21F-13

With over 13,500 aircraft built, the Mikoyan-Guryevich MiG-21 is the most widely produced combat aircraft of the cold war. It has served in 56 air forces and fought in more than thirty wars, including the Vietnam War, where it proved a capable opponent to U.S. fighters and bombers.

Designed as a short-range, clear-weather, supersonic fighter, the first production MiG-21F (F for *forsirovannyi*, or "afterburner") left the factory in late 1959. In 1960, the one-hundredth aircraft introduced the MiG-21F-13 series, equipped to launch heat-seeking K-13 air-to-air missiles. Light and agile, the F-13 would become the ultimate missile-armed MiG-21 dogfighter. Subsequent improvements to armament, fuel capacity, and electronics systems increased its weight.

The cockpit of the MiG-21F-13 was unpressurized, so pilots wore a partial-pressure anti-g suit and sealed helmet. A separate control on the right console heated the helmet for comfort and defrosted the faceplate. A clear, armored canopy/windscreen hinged forward for access from the ground; as the canopy closed, it depressed a plate behind the pilot's head, arming the ejection seat automatically. The canopy also hinged forward and left the aircraft with the seat to protect the pilot from wind blast during ejection.

MiG-21F pilots were guided toward their targets by ground controllers; pilots then intercepted targets visually—an operation complicated by the aircraft's poor visibility. A ranging radar was linked to the computing gun sight, with small lights warning when targets were still out of range. A thumb button at the left of the control stick steadied the gun sight's aiming reticle, while another below it operated the speed brakes. The index finger then fired the missiles or 30mm cannon.

The pilot's panel was relatively simple, lacking the large radar screens found on later MiG-21 variants. Avionics included an autopilot, automatic direction finder, radio altimeter, and radar warning receiver.

BEECH
KING AIR 65-90

The world's most popular turboprop aircraft, the Beech King Air has been a favorite of small companies since its introduction in 1964. The combination of Beech's earlier piston-engined Queen Air (more than 1,000 were built) with Pratt & Whitney Canada PT6 engines resulted in economical executive transport that remains in production more than 40 years after the first example was produced. With ceiling and range that are superior to similar piston-engined designs, the King Air can land safely on many runways considered too short for jet operation.

The aircraft depicted is a King Air 65-90, the designation applies to the 112 Model 65 Queen Air 88s constructed as, or modified to, Model 90 King Airs. Built in 1965, this King Air flew until 1998, when Beechcraft owner Raytheon delivered it to the National Air and Space Museum.

The passenger compartment (see page 117) was fully pressurized, with soundproofing to reduce cabin noise. The flight deck was accessible through an open bulkhead. Both pilots sat before complete flight instruments, with engine gauges shared on the center panel. Though easily within reach of either pilot, the wing-flap lever was placed to the left side of the center console, and the landing-gear lever was placed to the right. The fuel system was controlled from a console accessible only from the left seat. The center console managed engine speed and props, cabin pressure, elevator, aileron, and rudder trim tabs, with switches for the instrument landing system, radar altimeter, and autopilot. To switch on the battery prior to flight, the King Air 65-90 required a key, which was inserted into a lock on the main panel—similar to most of today's automobiles

THE NATIONAL AIR AND SPACE MUSEUM'S KING AIR 65-90,

SOON AFTER DELIVERY TO WASHINGTON, D.C., IN 1998.

THE NATIONAL AIR AND SPACE MUSEUM'S CONCORDE, DONATED BY AIR FRANCE,

IS NOW ON DISPLAY AT THE UDVAR-HAZY CENTER IN VIRGINIA.

AÉROSPATIALE/ BRITISH AIRCRAFT CORP CONCORDE

A technological marvel, Concorde was the only aircraft to sustain regularly scheduled passenger flights at twice the speed of sound. An Anglo-French joint venture, Concorde operated in Air France and British Airways liveries between January 1976 and November 2003.

When Concorde was designed, most world aircraft manufacturers had design studies for their own Supersonic Transport, or SST. As costs of development and production rose, most companies dropped out of contention. And as operating costs, environmental concerns, and passenger-comfort issues increased, airlines began to lose interest. The Soviet Union built and briefly operated a pair of Tu-144s; the press dubbed them Concordskis. Ultimately, the world SST fleet comprised 20 Concordes, of which only 14, all flown by British Airways and Air France, actually entered passenger service.

When delivered in the 1970s, Concorde offered its crews an advanced, if somewhat cramped, flight deck. It was the first airliner to employ analog fly-by-wire flight, engine, and wheel-brake controls. In addition to normal trim controls, the engineer could shift fuel between fuselage tanks to adjust the aircraft's center of gravity.

The pilot and engineer instrument panels were loaded with simple dials; plans to upgrade to a glass cockpit, with information on multifunctional displays, were shelved once it became clear that the SST would soon be leaving service.

Concorde's needle nose offered pilots extremely limited visibility, especially at landing, when the aircraft approached at a very high angle of attack. Engineers came up with a novel response to the problem; a lever on the front panel (see page 120) lowered the entire nose and provided an unobstructed view.

UP

VIS/0°

5°

DOWN

UP

VIS/0°

5°

DOWN

VISOR / NOSE

VISOR

NOSE

LH
SHORT

UPPER
LOCKS

RH
SHOR

AS SEEN HERE, THE BEDE BUILT BY PETER K. GRAICHEN AND ALBERT C. BECKWITH WAS ORIGINALLY A BD-5A, DISTINGUISHED BY ITS SHORT, 14-FOOT WINGSPAN. THE NATIONAL AIR AND SPACE MUSEUM LATER INSTALLED LONGER 21-FOOT WINGS, CHANGING THE DESIGNATION TO BD-5B.

BEDE BD-5B

To its credit, the BD-5B was one of the hottest and most innovative personal aircraft of the 1970s and 1980s. Tiny, with a fuselage length of only 13 feet and a wingspan of 21 feet, the BD-5 was a hit at air shows, where its zippy aerobatic performances thrilled both pilots and audiences. On the downside, the aircraft, as a homebuilt kitplane, was incredibly complex to form and assemble, with an overly complicated propulsion system—if an engine could even be found!

The design was the brainchild of gifted engineer James R. "Jim" Bede. Bede's BD-1, designed in 1961, became the first light aircraft manufactured with bonded aluminum construction. Unable to undertake mass production, Bede sold the design to the American Aviation Corporation, which built more than 1,700 examples as the AA-1. The BD-4 was a kitplane; buyers purchased components and materials, then formed and assembled the aircraft at home. About 600 BD-4 kits were sold.

In 1970 Bede began marketing a new, high-performance kitplane, the BD-5. Following the first flight in September 1971, 4,000 home-builders ordered kits, though few would ever fly. Several builders completed jet-propelled BD-5Js—at the time, the world's smallest aircraft—which was featured prominently in a number of air shows and motion pictures. But the BD-5 failed commercially, and Bede's first company went bankrupt in 1979. In 2005, Bede, who formed a new company to continue his design and production work, announced plans to put BD-5 back in development.

Fewer than 200 BD-5s ever flew. This example, built by Peter K. Graichen, took more than six years to complete. It first flew in October 1978, logging only about nine hours of flight time before Graichen and co-owner Albert C. Beckwith donated the aircraft to the National Air and Space Museum in 1984.

The pilot of the BD-5 stretched semi-recumbent beneath a plastic canopy and windscreen. Instrumentation, which varied with the individual builder, is quite advanced in Graichen and Beckwith's cockpit. On all BD-5s, the side-stick flight controller was very sensitive to pilot inputs.

Bell 206L-1 LongRanger II "Spirit of Texas"

Designed in the early 1960s as a light military observation helicopter, the Bell 206 JetRanger instead became a popular civil helicopter, finding roles in executive transport, traffic reporting, medical evacuation and airlift, border patrol, police support, forest-fire patrol and fire fighting, pilot training, and offshore supply. In 1973 Bell Helicopter introduced a new long-range, stretched version called the 206L-1 LongRanger II. More than 5,000 JetRangers and LongRangers have been produced in the U.S. and Italy.

In September 1982, a Model 206 flown by H. Ross Perot Jr. and Jay Coburn became the first helicopter to fly around the world. Departing from Fort Worth on September 1, the 206L-1 LongRanger II *Spirit of Texas* made the trip in just over 29 days. With a total flight time of more than 246 hours, Perot and Coburn averaged a ground speed of 117 miles per hour.

The *Spirit of Texas* was equipped with an additional internal 151-gallon fuel tank, raising endurance from three hours to eight. Floatation gear and survival equipment, which added to the takeoff weight, were a reassuring addition during the long hours over oceans, deserts, and jungles.

The JetRanger pilot sits in the right seat, standard practice in most of the world's helicopters. Flight instruments, though centered ahead of the pilot, are easily visible from the left seat, where a full set of controls allows the copilot to provide some relief. Helicopter autopilots, under development at the time of the round-the-world flight, are still a rarity. The full suite of navigational tools and radios at the left of the panel was state-of-the-art in 1982.

BELL LONGRANGER *SPIRIT OF TEXAS*, PHOTOGRAPHED SHORTLY AFTER ITS HISTORIC 1982 ROUND-THE-WORLD FLIGHT.

AFTER 70 YEARS, THE PEPSI SKYWRITER HAS FOUND A NEW HOME AT

THE NATIONAL AIR AND SPACE MUSEUM.

TRAVEL AIR D4D
"PEPSI SKYWRITER"

Skywriting, that most strenuous form of callig-raphy, became a popular form of advertising in the early 1920s. Pilots in acrobatic aircraft would trace patterns in the skies above cities, parks, or county fairs, using smoke generators to write their messages. An enthusiastic public, thrilling to the exuberant display of aeronautical prowess, was also encouraged to "Smoke Lucky Strikes," "Drink Pepsi Cola," or, on occasion, "Marry Me, Susie." The winds would soon erase the message, but the free air show was rarely forgotten.

More than 1,200 open-cockpit Travel Air biplanes were built between 1925 and 1930, when the Great Depression closed the company. Popular and made of sturdy wood and steel tubing with replaceable fabric, the Travel Airs were favorites with sportsman pilots, barnstormers (who could carry two passengers, sitting side by side in the front cockpit), crop dusters, and skywriters.

The aircraft that became the *Pepsi Skywriter* was built in 1929, then rebuilt as a Model D4D in 1930 with a more powerful engine and new shorter "Speed" wings. Andy Stinis, of the Skywriting Corporation of America, purchased the aircraft in 1931, contracting it to work for the Pepsi-Cola Corporation until 1953. Over that period, Pepsi, which also owned or contracted 13 additional aircraft, would become the firm responsible for more skywriting than any other advertiser.

Pepsi rediscovered the D4D, still owned by Andy Stinis, in 1973 and purchased it for display at corporate headquarters. But the 40-year-old Travel Air seemed more at home in flight; Pepsi executives agreed to upgrade the navigational and communications equipment and return the aircraft, now called the *Pepsi Skywriter*, to a national tour. Flown by Jack Strayer, Peggy Davies, Suzanne Asbury, and Steve Oliver, the *Pepsi Skywriter* continued its appearances around the country until 2000, by which time all agreed that safety would be best served if the aging aircraft were retired.

The *Pepsi Skywriter* remained an aircraft of the 1920s, but its upholstered open cockpit was sophis-ticated enough for the 1990s.

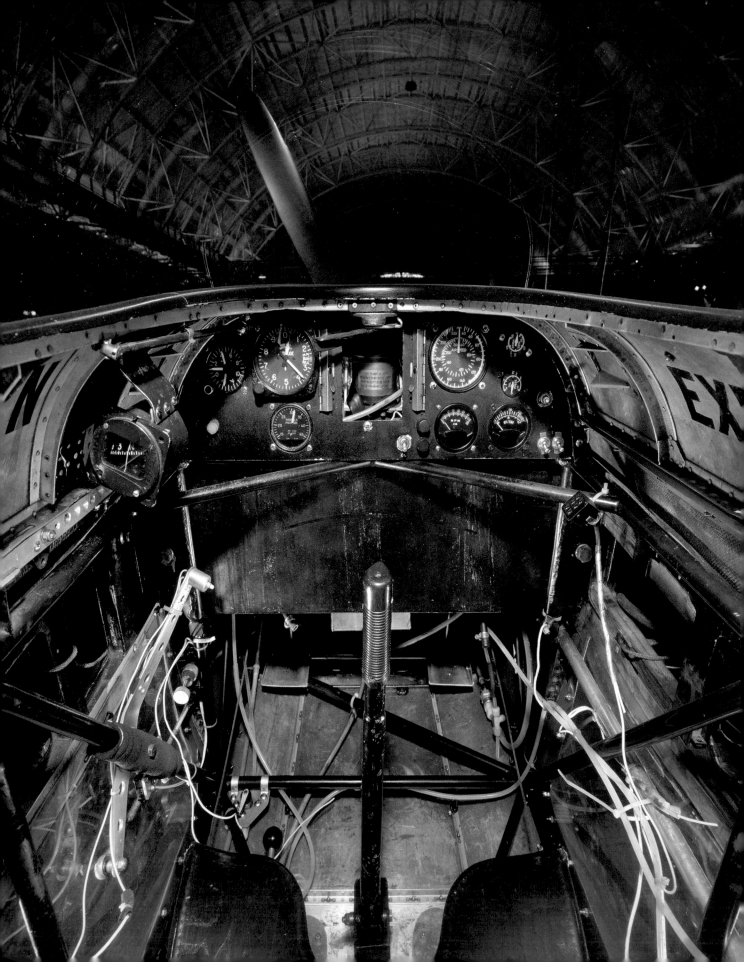

LOUDENSLAGER STEPHENS AKRO LASER 200

A natural aerobatic pilot and gifted designer, Leo Loudenslager engineered his Laser 200 for aerobatic competition. He built the aircraft in 1975, then flew it to win his first U.S. National Championship that year. Continuing to fly the Laser, Loudenslager went on to become the only seven-time national champion, repeating his win in 1976, 1977, 1978, 1980, 1981, and 1982. He also found the time to take the World Aerobatic Championship in 1980. Loudenslager retired from competition in 1983. Sponsored by Bud Light, he and the Laser 200 performed at air shows until his death in 1997.

Today, the Laser 200's data plate and registration identify it as a Stephens Akro, which is how the aircraft began life in the late 1960s. Loudenslager completed the kitplane in 1971, but he almost immediately began modifying it to improve its strength and aerobatic qualities. The 1975 redesign replaced everything but the fuselage aft of the pilot's seat. With the Nationals only months away, Loudenslager elected to leave the question of identity to some other time. But the Laser 200, more than the Stephens Akro, was the aircraft that influenced the next generation of aerobatic aircraft, including Walter Extra's dominant designs of the 1990s.

The Laser 200 cockpit appears deceptively incomplete, with wires and tubes snaking through the exposed steel-tube framing. Pilot comfort was of little concern in the design; routines were short, and the Laser was not designed for long, cross-country flights. The center of the instrument panel supported Loudenslager's script for each flight routine. Most instruments monitored engine performance, with an altimeter, airspeed indicator, accelerometer (the Laser's rugged structure could survive up to nine g's), and compass. With no artificial horizon, Loudenslager remainded aware of his ever-changing attitude through a single-piece, clear-vision canopy and Plexiglas windows on either side of the cockpit beneath the wings.

LEO LOUDENSLAGER
IN HIS LASER 200,
PHOTOGRAPHED DURING HIS
AIR SHOW CAREER.

BELL XV-15 TILT ROTOR RESEARCH AIRCRAFT

It is too early to properly judge the historical significance of the Bell XV-15 Tilt Rotor Research Aircraft. The development of vertical takeoff and landing (VTOL) technology has been a dream for centuries. Part of that dream was realized in the 1930s with the invention of the helicopter, an aircraft that could take off and land vertically, albeit with limited forward speed and range. Developed in the 1960s, small, ducted thrust VTOL jets (such as the British Harrier) offered greatly improved top speeds, but the technology was not practical for larger transports. Tilt Rotor technology, developed with the National Aeronautics and Space Administration (NASA), allows an aircraft to take off like a helicopter then convert to forward flight with the efficiency of an airplane. As developed by the Bell XV-15, the Tilt Rotor may one day be as common as the helicopter.

The XV-15 Tilt Rotor, which first flew in May 1977, derives its power from two turboshaft engines driving massive, 25-foot-diameter, three-bladed propellers. Hydraulic gears rotate the engines and props vertically for takeoff, landing, or hovering. Rotated 90 degrees, the props produce forward thrust, while the 32-foot wings create lift. The XV-15 test program was completed in 2003, but the technology continues to be developed in several projects. Bell and the Italian firm Agusta are designing the Bell/Agusta BA609 civil executive transport, while Bell and Boeing are producing larger V-22 Ospreys for the U.S. military. Bell is working on a smaller unmanned reconnaissance vehicle called Eagle Eye, and the U.S. Marines have shown interest in a small, manned gunship.

The XV-15's pilots sat in ejection seats in an unpressurized cockpit. The pilot was seated on the right, the normal position for helicopter pilots, and both pilots flew using helicopter-style controls. By pulling up on a power lever with the left hand, the pilot increased rotor pitch and engine rpm for vertical takeoff; a small thumb switch then articulated the props and engines forward for the normal cruise setting. In the event of an engine failure, a clutch system automatically divided power from the surviving engine between both props. In the event of a hydraulic failure, a backup system could switch to the vertical flight mode for a normal landing. The co-pilot's glass cockpit multifunction display, showed the same information as the many gauges mounted in front of the pilot.

"BREITLING ORBITER 3"

On March 21, 1999, Bertrand Piccard and Bryan Jones piloted *Breitling Orbiter 3* to a desert landing in western Egypt, thus completing the first global circumnavigation by a free balloon. Balloon navigation is a skill that has been developing for two and a half centuries. Over any given spot on earth, winds travel in different directions at different altitudes. The balloonist must first find the appropriate wind, then rise or descend to that altitude, riding the current until another change is required.

The first round-the-world flight was proposed in 1980. Over the next two decades, seven teams attempted the flight 16 times. Sponsored by Breitling SA, makers of fine Swiss chronometers, Piccard and Wim Verstaeten tried unsuccessfully in 1997 and 1998. For the third attempt, using the new *Breitling Orbiter 3* gondola and balloon envelope, Bryan Jones was replaced with Verstaeten. Piccard and Jones left Switzerland on March 1, 1999, their flight lasting almost 20 days and covering 25,361 miles.

Helium gas, the primary source of buoyancy in most long-distance balloons, eventually migrates through every fabric used for envelope design. To minimize helium loss, *Breitling Orbiter 3* used a dense inner membrane supported by nylon fabric, with an aluminized outer skin to improve thermal control. Propane heaters warmed the helium, providing additional lift at night to prevent cooling and the loss of altitude.

Piccard and Jones worked in a sealed gondola built from Kevlar and carbon-fiber cloth. Supplemental oxygen was carried in tanks, and filters scrubbed carbon dioxide from the cabin atmosphere. Solar panels provided electrical power, stored in batteries. Cabin temperature was generally a cool 59 degrees Fahrenheit, though it occasionally dipped below freezing. The control station provided flight data, links to satellite systems (particularly helpful for tracking weather patterns), and communications equipment to maintain contact with the outside world. The civil Swiss registration, HB-BRA, was used as the radio call sign.

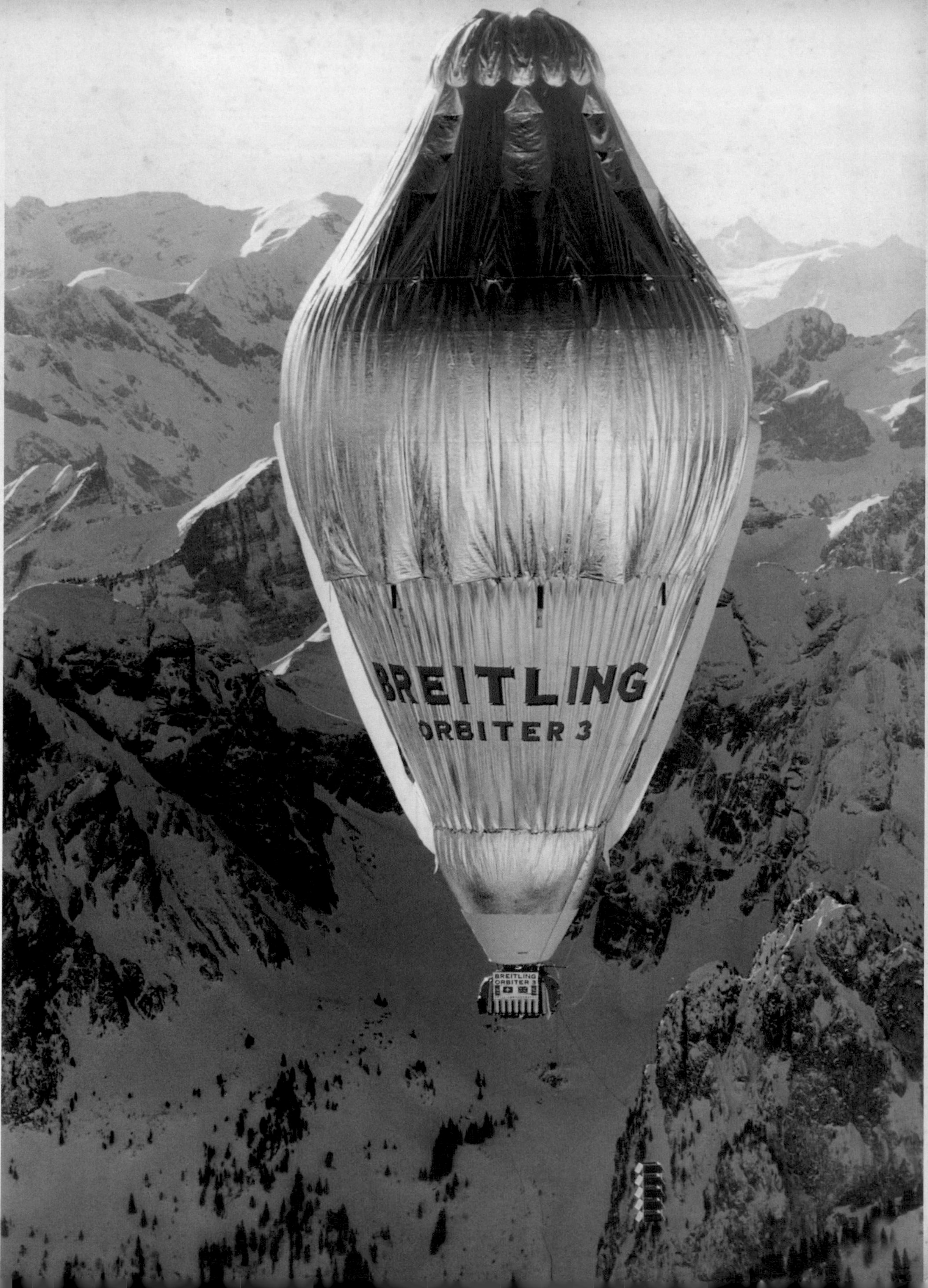
BREITLING
ORBITER 3

LEFT: PHOTOGRAPHED OVER THE ALPS, THE BREITLING ORBITER 3 BEGINS ITS ROUND-THE-WORLD JOURNEY.

ABOVE: BERTRAND PICCARD AND BRYAN JONES WAVE FROM ATOP THE BREITLING ORBITER 3 GONDOLA,

FOLLOWING THE HISTORIC ARTIFACT'S INSTALLATION AT THE NATIONAL AIR AND SPACE MUSEUM.

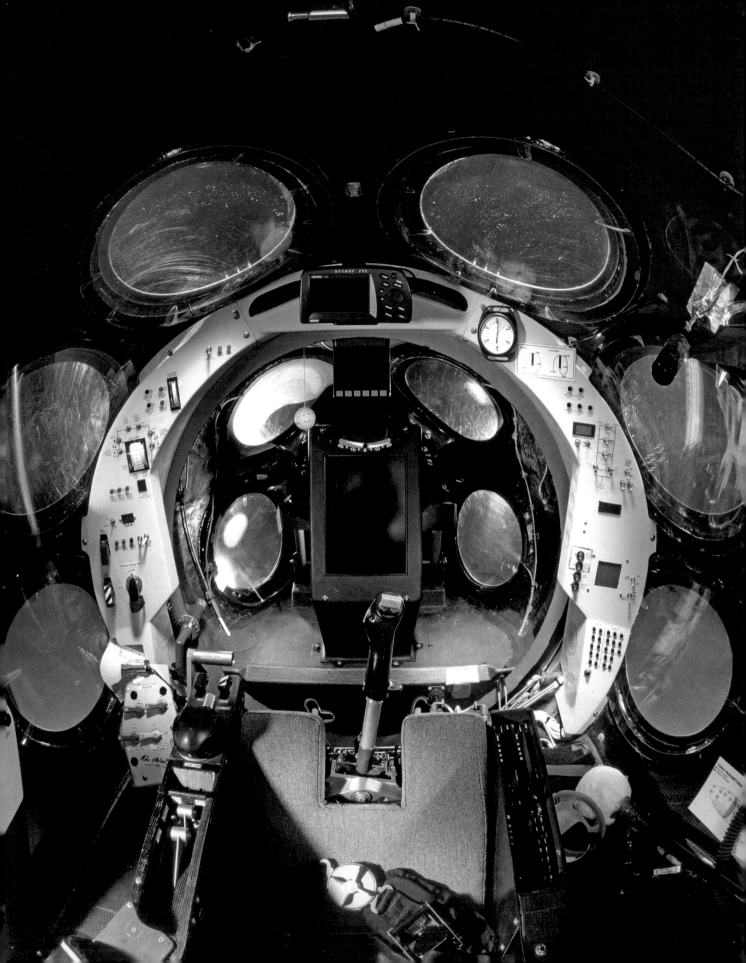

SCALED COMPOSITES MODEL 316 "SPACESHIPONE"

Government-sponsored, human spaceflight has been a reality since 1961, but the first privately sponsored space flight would have to wait more than four decades. On June 21, 2004, pilot Mike Melvill flew the privately sponsored *SpaceShipOne* to an altitude above 100,000 meters (or 328,000 feet, the officially recognized beginning of space) and returned safely to a desert landing strip at Mojave, California. During its test program, *SpaceShipOne* also became the first privately funded aircraft to exceed Mach 2 and Mach 3.

Financed by Microsoft cofounder Paul G. Allen, *SpaceShipOne* was designed and built by Burt Rutan's company, Scaled Composites, as Model 316, a reusable space test vehicle. Rutan also designed a more conventional spacecraft, the *White Knight* mother plane, which carried the spacecraft to launch altitude. At 46,000 feet, *SpaceShipOne* dropped away, fired its rocket engine, and turned toward space.

The impetus for the development of this remarkable aircraft was the Ansari X Prize, a $10 million award to the first private aircraft to reach 100 km twice in two weeks. No more than 10 percent of the nonfuel weight could be replaced between flights, and the craft had to carry the equivalent of three people.

On September 29, 2004, Mike Melvill made the first X Prize flight (his second space flight), with ballast in the two passenger seats. Six days later, on October 4, Brian Binnie made the second X Prize flight (his first space flight), winning the X Prize for *SpaceShipOne* and its team.

SpaceShipOne made 17 flights (six of them under its own power, and three of those into space) before retiring to the National Air and Space Museum. British executive Sir Richard Branson, through his new company Virgin Galactic, is now committed to fund the development of *SpaceShipTwo*, with a plan to provide private passenger service to outer space.

The cockpits of *SpaceShipOne* and *White Knight* are laid out identically. Both are fully pressurized. Pilots of the spacecraft flew with flight helmets and oxygen masks, but no pressure suits were worn. Few instruments were carried, with all flight and systems information displayed in a central multifunction display (MFD). A couple of items in *SpaceShipOne*'s cockpit were decidedly low-tech: a suspended Ping-Pong ball (page 138, bottom) marked the onset of zero gravity, while a stick with a fuzzy ball at the end (page 138, top) mopped condensation from the many circular windows.

SPACESHIPONE (FOREGROUND) WAS DELIVERED TO

THE NATIONAL AIR AND SPACE MUSEUM BY MOTHERSHIP WHITE KNIGHT.

PHOTOGRAPHY CREDITS

WRIGHT BROTHERS 1903 FLYER
12 SI 2006-23887.44 14 SI 2003-19429 15 SI 79-759

WRIGHT BROTHERS 1909 MILITARY FLYER
16 SI 2006-20911 17 SI 2006-20918

CURTISS MODEL D HEADLESS PUSHER
18 SI 2006-20900 19 SI 79-13575

ECKER FLYING BOAT
20 SI 2006-21267 21 SI 82-8329

HALBERSTADT CL.IV
22 SI 2006-20907 23 SI 2005-24666

FOKKER T-2
24 SI 2006-21266 25 SI 92-932 (COURTESY OF FAIRCHILD)

ARROW SPORT A2-60
26 SI 2005-2498 28 SI 2006-22803 29 SI 2006-22804

LOCKHEED 5B VEGA "LITTLE RED BUS"
30 SI 2006-21920
31 SI 80-2082 (PHOTO BY DANE PENLAND)

MONOCOUPE 110 SPECIAL "LITTLE BUTCH"
32 SI 2005-2488 33 SI 87-9653

BÜCKER BÜ 133 C JUNGMEISTER
34 SI 2005-2485 35 SI 85-16341

NAVAL AIRCRAFT FACTORY N3N-3
36 SI 2005-2489
37 SI 2006-20923 (RUDY ARNOLD PHOTO COLLECTION)

PIPER J-3C CUB
38 SI 2005-2493
39 SI 2006-20919 (HANS GROENHOFF PHOTO COLLECTION)

TURNER-LAIRD LTR-14 "MISS CHAMPION"
40 SI 2006-20915
42/43 SI 90-4835 (RUDY ARNOLD PHOTO COLLECTION)

WESTLAND LYSANDER MARK III
44 SI 2005-4072 45 SI 2006-20917

BOEING S-307 STRATOLINER "CLIPPER FLYING CLOUD"
46 SI 2006-20909 47 SI 2006-29070
48 SI 72-3667 49 SI 2006-20910

HAWKER HURRICANE MARK IIC
50 SI 2006-20906 51 SI 91-7087

CURTISS P-40E-1 WARHAWK/KITTYHAWK MARK IA
52 SI 2005-2483
53 SI 2006-20920 (HANS GROENHOFF PHOTO COLLECTION)

FRANKFORT TG-1A
54 SI 2005-2484 55 SI 2006-20916

VOUGHT F4U-1D CORSAIR
56 SI 2005-2481 57 SI 80-17164 58/59 SI 2006-6855

STINSON L-5 SENTINEL
60 SI 2005-2487 61 SI 2006-20921

MARTIN B-26B MARAUDER "FLAK BAIT"
62 SI 2006-21269
64 SI 2006-20922 (RUDY ARNOLD PHOTO COLLECTION)
65 SI 2006-21270

Messerschmitt Bf 109 G-6
66 SI 98-15195 67 SI 74-4297

Lockheed P-38J Lightning
68 SI 2006-20914 69 SI 94-13960 (Lockheed Martin)

Republic P-47D-30 Thunderbolt
70 SI 2006-20905 71 SI 87-750

de Havilland D.H.98 Mosquito TT Mark 35
72 SI 2006-20908 73 SI 72-8523

Grumman F6F-3 Hellcat
74 SI 2005-2492
75 SI 2006-20938 (Rudy Arnold Photo Collection)

Kawasaki Ki-45 Kai Hei Toryu
76 SI 2006-21850 77 SI 2006-21923

Dornier Do 335 Pfeil
78 SI 2006-20902 79 (left) SI 76-1950
79 (right) SI 2006-29071

Junkers Ju 388 L-1
80 SI 2006-20912 82 SI 2006-20932 83 SI 2006-20913

Heinkel He 219 Uhu
84 SI 2006-20903 85 SI 2006-20931
86 (left) SI 2006-21961 86 (right) SI 2006-21852
87 SI 2006-20904

Lockheed XP-80 Shooting Star "Lulu-Belle"
88 SI 98-15876
89 SI 2006-20940 (Rudy Arnold Photo Collection)

Lockheed T-33A Shooting Star
90 SI 2006-21847 92 United States Air Force
93 SI 2006-21851

North American FJ-1 Fury
94 SI 2006-21922 95 SI 94-4093

Piper PA-18 Super Cub
96 SI 2005-2499 97 SI 2006-20935

Schweizer SGU 2-22EK
98 SI 2005-2486 99 SI 2006-22808

de Havilland-Canada DHC-1A Chipmunk "Pennzoil Special"
100 SI 2005-2495 101 SI 2004-18518

Mikoyan-Guryevich MiG-15bis (J-2)
102 SI 2006-21846 103 SI 83-9139

Boeing 367-80
104 SI 2005-4070 105 SI 2006-22805

Martin EB-57B Canberra
106 SI 2006-21963 107 United States Air Force

McDonnell F4H-1 (F-4A) Phantom II "Sageburner"
108 SI 2006-21921 109 United States Navy
110 SI 2006-21849 111 United States Navy

Mikoyan-Guryevich MiG-21F-13
112 SI 2006-21848 113 SI 2006-21725

Beech King Air 65-90
114 SI 2006-23885 116 SI 99-15069.8 117 SI 2006-23886

Aérospatiale/British Aircraft Corp Concorde
118 SI 2005-4060 119 SI 2005-6277
120 SI 2006-29072 121 SI 2005-4060

Bede BD-5B
122 SI 2005-2490 123 SI 2006-20927

Bell 206L-1 LongRanger II "Spirit of Texas"
124 SI 98-16041 125 SI 95-3642

Travel Air D4D "Pepsi Skywriter"
126 SI 2005-2496 127 SI 2006-22807

Loudenslager Stephens Akro Laser 200
128 SI 2005-2497 129 SI 2006-20926

Bell XV-15 Tilt Rotor Research Aircraft
130 SI 2006-236 131 SI 2003-44812

"Breitling Orbiter 3"
132 SI 2006-21268 133 SI 2006-20925
134 SI 2006-21451 135 SI 2003-5519

Scaled Composites Model 316 "SpaceShipOne"
136 SI 2005-24511 138 (top) SI 2006-23580
138 (bottom) SI 2006-23581 139 SI 2005-24511

Photographers/Author photograph by Caroyln Russo
142

FROM LEFT TO RIGHT: PHOTOGRAPHERS ERIC F. LONG AND MARK A. AVINO AND AUTHOR DANA BELL.

ACKNOWLEDGMENTS

Any book requires a great deal of support. Eric, Mark, and Dana would like to thank the following individuals and organizations:

At the National Air and Space Museum (NASM), this project was backed by the front office, particularly Director Gen. John Dailey (USMC, Ret.), Deputy Director Col. Don Lopez (USAF, Ret), and Assistant Director Dr. Ted Maxwell. The Museum's capable Publications Officer, Trish Graboske, managed much of the preparatory work and liaison.

Effective coordination and support came from NASM's Communications Director Claire Brown and Public Affairs Specialist Mike Marcus, who helped keep us on track.

The work of preparing the aircraft for photography and protecting them during our work was handled by the staff of the Collections Division. These folks also provided valuable insight into the conditions of the aircraft they had restored as we prepared our lists of subjects. In particular, we would like to thank Collections Division Chief Elizabeth Garcia, Preservation and Restoration Unit Chief Richard Kowalczyk, and staff members Tony Karp, Karl Heinzel, Ed Mautner, Rob Mawhinney, John Shatz, Scott Wiley, Dave Wilson, and Scott Wood.

NASM's archival images and documents are protected and managed by the Archives Division. We appreciate the always-cordial support of that staff, particularly Chief Marilyn Graskowiak, and Dan Hagedorn, Kate Igoe, Mark Kahn, Kristine L. Kaske-Martin, Melissa A. N. Keiser, Paul Silbermann, David Schwartz, and Larry Wilson.

Support interpreting the collections and aircraft came from the Department of Aeronautics, chaired by Peter Jakab. Most of the curators helped it one way or another, and we would like to thank Dorothy Cochrane, Roger Connor, Dr. Tom Crouch, Dr. Dik Daso, Russell E. Lee, Dr. Dominick A. Pisano, and Dr. Bob van der Linden.

NASM photographer Dane Penland was always there to support this project or supply a needed image.

At the Smithsonian Institution, this book benefited from the support of Ellen Nanney at Smithsonian Business Ventures and Caroline Newman at SI Books.

The staff at HarperCollins Publishers took our project and created this book. We are indebted to Elizabeth Viscott Sullivan, Will Staehle, Dinah Fried, Ilana Anger, Donna Sanzone, Marta Schooler, Carol Reed, and Margarita Vaisman.

We are honored that John Travolta, a skilled aviator and longtime friend of the National Air and Space Museum wrote the foreword to our book. Highly regarded in the aviation community for his abilities as a pilot, he is rated to fly a variety of jet aircraft, including the 747.

Much of the time spent on this project would have otherwise been spent with our families. We particularly appreciate the support and understanding of our wives, Kathy, Laurene, and Susan.